MW01039018

Mud and Water

MUD AND WATER

THE COLLECTED TEACHINGS OF
ZEN MASTER BASSUI

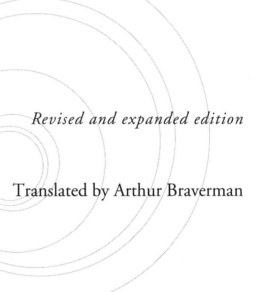

Revised and expanded edition

Translated by Arthur Braverman

WISDOM PUBLICATIONS • BOSTON

Wisdom Publications
199 Elm Street
Somerville, MA 02144 USA
www.wisdompubs.org

© 2002 Arthur Braverman
All rights reserved.

No part of this book may be reproduced in any form or by any means,
electronic or mechanical, including photography, recording, or by any
information storage and retrieval system or technologies now known
or later developed, without permission in writing from the publisher.

Library of Congress Cataloging-in-Publication Data
Bassui Tokushō, 1327–1387
  [Enzan wadei gassuishū. English]
  Mud and water : the collected teachings of Zen Master Bassui /
Translated by Arthur Braverman.
      p.   cm.
  Includes index.
  ISBN 0-86171-320-6 (alk. paper)
    1. Spiritual life—Zen Buddhism—Early works to 1800. 2. Zen
Buddhism—Doctrines—Early works to 1800. I. Braverman,
Arthur, 1942– II. Title.
  BQ9288.B3713 2002
  294.3'444—dc21   2002007164

ISBN 0-86171-320-6

First Wisdom Edition

06 05 04 03 02

5   4   3   2   1

Cover by Richard Snizik
Interior by Stephanie Doyle
Cover photograph, "Woods," by Gary Irving (Photodisc).

Wisdom Publications' books are printed on acid-free
paper and meet the guidelines for the permanence and
durability of the Production Guidelines for Book Long-
evity of the Council on Library Resources.

Printed in Canada

To the memory of Sophie Braverman and Joe Rubin

Table of Contents

Part I

Part II

PART III

Acknowledgments

Thanks to Ralph Edsell, Anne Forer, Peter Haskel, Doug Honeyman, Surya Dass Miller, Richard Kortum, and Hanalore Rosset for reading sections of the translation and offering many useful suggestions; to Professor Kiyoshi Hoshi for the use of his photographs relating to Bassui's life and for making his comprehensive research on Bassui available to me; to Ichiro Shirato Sensei for teaching me how to read Japanese; to Hiroko Sanada Braverman for answering countless questions regarding difficult passages in the text; and to our daughter, Nao, for her ability to understand from age two that when Daddy is at the typewriter, it is time to find another playmate.

Preface to the New Edition

IT HAS BEEN over ten years since the publication of the translation of Bassui's *Enzanwadeigassui-shū*. When Josh Bartok from Wisdom Publications asked me if I had any books no longer in print, I immediately thought of a new and expanded addition of the teachings of Bassui. The record of Bassui's teaching was my first published translation of Japanese classical Zen texts and still my most cherished. The *Enzanwadeigassui-shū* published under the English title of *Mud and Water* is the most comprehensive text of Bassui's talks. Still, there is more to this unique Zen figure. With the addition of some of his letters to monks, nuns, and laypersons and his talk on questioning your mind, we get a more complete picture of Bassui's teachings. The extensive research on Bassui by the late Professor Kiyoshi Hoshi has helped me greatly in revising this translation. Finally I would like to thank Diana and Richard St. Ruth, publishers of *Buddhism Now* for their generous support of my work in general and for letting me use the Bassui letters I'd previously published in *Buddhism Now*.

Arthur Braverman
Ojai, California
1/21/02

Introduction

THE ENZANWADEIGASSUI-SHŪ *(A Collection of Mud and Water from Enzan,* hereafter referred to as the *Wadegassui)* is a series of talks between the fourteenth-century Zen master Bassui Tokushō and his disciples—monks, nuns, and laypeople. Since it records the questions of his disciples and Bassui's responses to them, these are not Dharma talks in the formal sense, but rather the informal teaching of Bassui as he responds to the questions of his disciples in an attempt to clear up their doubts. Sometimes his responses are short, direct, and spontaneous. At other times he seems to use the question as a springboard to crucial aspects of the teaching. Through these exchanges we see not only the teaching method of a mature Zen master, but also the religious beliefs and superstitions held by four-teenth-century Japanese at a time when Japan was afflicted by civil war. Though the disciples' backgrounds were diverse and their per-spectives quite varied, Bassui always managed to bring the students back to what he considered the essence of Zen: seeing into one's own nature. Bassui's ability to connect these diverse questions to this central theme in Zen and to make the complex Buddhist doc-trines comprehensible to monks and laypersons is what makes him unique as a Zen master.

Bassui uses illustrative examples when questioned about popu-lar sutras of the time. When queried about sections of the *Lotus Sutra,* the *Amida Sutra,* and the *Sutra of the Bodhisattva Jizō,* he shows how they all express the one teaching: "Seeing into one's own nature is Buddhahood." Indeed, he reduces the Six Perfections of the Prajñāpāramitā Sutra to this one truth. Moreover, his verbal acrobatics are always coupled with a true passion, which would impress upon his disciples the urgent need to look into their own nature. And it is this ability to express his understanding with such clarity and passion that drew monks and laypeople to him in droves.

When asked how one goes about seeing into his own nature, Bassui would ask the student to inquire into the one who is asking the question—"the one who is speaking right now." This approach did not originate with Bassui. But here again it is Bassui's way of focusing on this one question to the exclusion of all else that gives his Zen its unique flavor. And since Bassui himself had been tormented by this question throughout his life as a seeker, it is perhaps not surprising that it was to become the central theme of his teaching. To understand the foundation from which this teaching grew, we should first look into Bassui's life and practice up to the time he became the mature teacher we see in the *Wadeigassui*.

Bassui's Life

Bassui Tokushō was born in Nakamura, a district in the province of Sagami, in what is now Kanagawa prefecture, in 1327, on the sixth day of the tenth month.[1] His family name was Fujiwara, but there seems to be no record of the given names of either his father or his mother. He was born during the reign of the Emperor Godaigo (1318–1339), a period when the Hōjō, a military family that virtually ruled over Japan for more than a hundred years, was losing its control over the country. At this time Japan was on the verge of a civil war that would last more than fifty years.

Bassui's mother was said to have had a dream that she would give birth to a demon child. Unable to shake off the fear of this omen, she abandoned the newborn Bassui in a nearby field. A family servant found the child there, took him in, and raised him.[2] When Bassui was four years old, his father died. Three years later, at a memorial service for him, Bassui asked the attending priest how his father could eat the offerings placed on the altar. When told that it was his father's soul that would eat the offerings, he asked, "What is this thing called a soul?" This was the beginning of an inquiry that Bassui was to pursue throughout most of his life. At around nine years old he was horrified by talk of the agonies of the three evil paths.[3] He then inquired more deeply into the meaning of soul. After some years, this investigation led him to another question: "Who is the one who sees, hears, and understands?" For long periods of time he sat in meditation, forgetting his own body, until one day he realized there was nothing one could grasp to call the soul. With this new view of the emptiness of all things, Bassui no longer felt the burden of body and mind, and his doubts about the Buddhadharma (the truth; the teaching of the Buddha), for the time being, were cleared up.

This period of tranquillity continued until one day he read in a popular book, "The mind is host, the body is guest." Once more doubts began to arise in Bassui. If the mind is host, he thought, then all cannot be void. This host must be the master who sees, hears, and understands that all things are empty. But who then is this master? He could not free himself of this new doubt.

At around twenty years of age Bassui went to study under the Zen master Ōkō at Jifukuji Temple in his home province, Sagami. He did not shave his head and become a monk, however, until he was twenty-nine. When he did at last officially become a monk, he had little taste for ritual and rejected the superstitions that clothed so many of the religious institutions of his time. He neither wore robes nor recited sutras like other monks. He simply practiced meditation in an uncompromising fashion, oblivious to wind, rain, and cold. This was to be Bassui's way throughout his life as a Zen practitioner.

Friendship with Tokukei

There was a monk from Bassiu's hometown by the name of Tokukei Jisha who had cut himself off from the world, retiring to the mountains, practicing religious austerities for many years. Hearing of this monk, Bassui decided to pay him a visit. Tokukei, seeing Bassui with head shaved and in laymen's clothes, asked suspiciously, "Why don't you wear monk's robes?"

Bassui: I became a monk to understand the great matter of life and death, not to wear Buddhist robes.

Tokukei: I see. Then are you looking into the kōans of the old masters?

Bassui: Of course not. How can I appreciate the words of others when I don't even know my own mind?

Tokukei: Well, then, how do you approach your religious practice?

Bassui: Having become a monk, I want to clarify the source of the great Dharma handed down by the buddhas and the ancestors. After attaining enlightenment, I want to save the bright and the dull, teaching each one according to his capacity. My true desire is to relieve others of their pain though I myself may fall into hell.

Hearing this Tokukei simply put his palms together and bowed. A friendship grew between these two monks from that time.

Bassui vowed not to preach a word of the Dharma to others until he received certification of his own realization from a true teacher. Once he received such certification, he would devote his life to saving others. To fulfill this vow he practiced harder than ever, telling himself this doubting mind is after all empty. He carried this investigation as far as he could without any real clarification. Then, one day, after sitting in meditation through the night, the sound of the mountain stream at dawn penetrated his whole body and Bassui suddenly had a realization.

He then went in search of a teacher to verify his understanding. Hearing of a well-known Zen master, Kōzan Mongo at Kenchōji Temple in Kamakura, Bassui set out to see him. Kōzan confirmed Bassui's understanding. This was sometime in the second month of the year 1358, when Bassui was thirty-one years old. It was at this time that he started wearing Buddhist robes and began making pilgrimages around the country visiting Zen masters.

Bassui went to see Fukuan Sōki, of Hōunji Temple in Hitachi province, a noted Zen master who had studied in China. Fukuan had a following that numbered about two thousand. Bassui, unimpressed with Fukuan, returned to his hometown and went to see his friend Tokukei. He told Tokukei that he had not got on well with Fukuan and was planning to practice by himself in some isolated mountain retreat. Tokukei, having spent over twenty years practicing austerities in seclusion, had developed a great deal of pride in his practice. This pride became the cause of much of his pain and suffering. He warned Bassui of the dangers of this kind of seclusion before fully understanding "the great matter" or receiving the transmission from a true teacher.[4] Though Bassui had received verification from Kōzan, he gave up the idea of secluding himself in the mountains in accord with his friend's advice and instead spent that year in a summer and winter training *sesshin* with Tokukei. Tokukei told Bassui of a certain Kohō Kakumyō, of Unjuji Temple in Izumo, who was considered a truly great teacher. Bassui soon set out for Unjuji.

Meeting with Kohō

Kohō Kakumyō (1271–1361) was a Dharma heir to the national teacher Hattō (Shinchi Kakushin, 1227–1298), who brought the Dharma transmitted through Mumon Ekai, the compiler of the

famous Zen classic collection of kōans, the *Mumonkan,* back to
Japan. Shinchi had studied esoteric Buddhism of the Shingon sect on
Mount Kōya, and then studied Zen under Dōgen (1200–1253),
founder of the Japanese Sōtō sect, and Enni Bennen (1202–1280)
before going to China. His disciple Kohō also studied for a while in
China with the great Chinese Zen master Chūhō Myōhon.[5] Kohō,
who received the bodhisattva precepts from Keizan Jōkin, the fourth
ancestor in the Japanese Sōtō line, was a strict teacher who greatly val-
ued the precepts. He did not confirm Bassui's understanding right
away, however, but asked him to stay awhile at Unjuji Temple. Bassui stayed on, but as was his custom he declined to reside on the temple grounds. He lived in a nearby hut and visited the master daily.

One day during their meeting Kohō asked Bassui why Jōshū
responded to the kōan "Does a dog have Buddha-nature?" with the
one word *mu* ("no"). Bassui answered with the verse:

> Mountains, rivers, and the great earth,
> Grass, trees, and the forests,
> All are mu.

When Kohō reprimanded him for responding with his rational
mind, Bassui felt as though the foundation of his body and mind fell
off like the bottom falling off a barrel. He expressed his experience
in this poem:

> Six windows naturally open, a cold lone flower,
> Unju[6] strikes the rubbish from my eyes,
> Crushes the gem in my hand right before me,
> So be it, this gold has become hard iron.

Bassui's profound awakening pointed out to him how narrow his
previous view of emptiness was. Kohō verified his understanding and

gave him the name Bassui, meaning far above average. Bassui was thirty-two years old.

After only two months at Unjuji Temple, Bassui once again took to the road seeking out Zen masters to engage in Dharma talk. He was asked to stay on to receive the bodhisattva precepts, which Kohō had received from Keizan Jōkin. Bassui, having little fondness for the ceremony connected with temples, decided to move on. His desire to seclude himself in a mountain retreat in order to deepen his understanding remained alive.

Bassui left Unjuji Temple and called upon a well-known Zen master named Dōzen from Inaba. Unimpressed with Dōzen, Bassui returned to his friend Tokukei. He told Tokukei of his stay with Kohō and described Kohō's Zen to him. Tokukei, happy for his friend, told him of his own regrets at not having met such a teacher in his youth. He said that being an old man he had lost the chance of ever meeting someone like Kohō.

It was around this time that Bassui built his first hermitage in Nanasawa in his home province, Sagami. Tokukei came to visit him there, and this time he seemed pleased with Bassui's decision to retire to a hermitage to continue his practice. He seemed to be telling Bassui that since he now had met both requirements—having clarified the Way and having received verification from a true teacher—he was ready to undertake this kind of practice.

Bassui had a dream that his old teacher, Kohō, was near death. He went to visit Kohō at Daiyūji, the temple he had founded and where he was now residing. After paying his respects to Kohō and seeing his poor condition, Bassui wanted to stay on with him. He left, however, for reasons uncertain but perhaps related to strained relations with some long-standing disciples of the teacher. The older disciples may have resented Bassui's decision to live off the temple grounds when he first studied under Kohō. Some were perhaps jealous that Bassui had received the transmission from Kohō after such a short stay with him. All this resentment may have been compounded by the fact that Bassui did not mix with the other monks and refused to take part in the formal temple activities during his short stay at Unjuji. Kohō died in 1361 in his ninety-first year. Bassui himself was then thirty-five.

Meetings with Other Zen Masters

That same year, Bassui moved to a hermitage in the province of Ki. On the way he stopped off at Eigenji Temple in the province of Gō to meet Jakushitsu Genkō. Jakushitsu, a well-known Zen master, had been to China and had also studied with Chūhō Myōhon. Bassui was attracted to the elegant simplicity of Jakushitsu's Zen. They talked about the meaning of monastic life and of Bassui's practice before his formal ordination. Bassui spoke to the monks at Eigenji. He told them that the meaning of monkhood was not to recite sutras but rather to put their lives in order. Bassui always seemed to warn against the dangers of excessive formalization so prevalent in the great religious institutions of the time. In his own life he preferred small hermitages to large monasteries. In his later years when he lived at his temple, Kōgakuan, at Enzan, he refused invitations to take charge of Daiyūji Temple and Unjuji Temple, the two large monasteries connected with his teacher Kohō.

After leaving Jakushitsu, Bassui returned to the province of Ki to a retreat on Mount Sudayama. A learned monk by the name of Chikugan Teizōsu, who had studied for a long time under Kohō, lived on a nearby mountain. Chikugan and Bassui had long talks. When Bassui had a problem understanding something in the Blue Cliff Record or the Record of Lin-chi, he would discuss it with Chikugan. Chikugan is recorded to have said that he never met anyone who studied the Way as did Bassui; indeed, he said, Bassui had left him far behind.

The following year Bassui went to visit the renowned Zen master of the Sōtō sect, Gasan Jōseki,[7] at Eikōji Temple. Bassui was very critical of the Rinzai practice of studying kōans, perhaps because they were becoming more and more formalized, hence losing their original spirit. He seems to have been attracted to the Sōtō sect for its stress on being attentive to all one's everyday activities. After observing the monks at Eikōji Temple, where Gasan was in charge, Bassui developed reservations about the monks there with their tendency toward idealization. He did, however, respect the master and stayed to study with him. Gasan approved of Bassui's understanding, but Bassui, in his usual fashion, refused to stay on to receive the transmission of Gasan's line.

From Hermitage to Hermitage

Bassui spent the next seventeen years moving around the country living in many hermitages. Though he never stayed more than three years in any one place, a following of devotees began to grow around him. When the numbers got too great, he even went so far as to leave a hermitage secretly and relocate somewhere else. It was not until his final years at his hermitage, the Kōgakuan, that he seemed ready to accept disciples in large numbers.

Kōgakuan: Bassui's Final Years

In 1378, Bassui moved to a hermitage on Mount Takemori in the province of Kai. The number of disciples kept increasing; indeed, the records show that eight hundred devotees gathered there. Because of the steep mountain path and the strong winds, Bassui was encouraged to move to the hermitage in Enzan. This was the famous hermitage, the Kōgakuan, where Bassui was to remain for the rest of his days. The year was 1380. At this point, it is clear that Bassui was ready to accept the role of teacher of a large institution. Though he refused the abbotship of two large monasteries and kept the final character *an* at the end of Kōgakuan (referring to it as a hermitage rather than a monastery), he accepted all who came to study with him. The number grew to over a thousand monks and lay devotees.

It was at Kōgakuan that the *Wadeigassui* was recorded. It was published in 1386—a year before Bassui's death—not at Bassui's request but with his permission. In his final years he developed great faith in the bodhisattva Kannon, the Bodhisattva of Compassion (Avalokiteśvara in Sanskrit). The name Kannon is the shortened form of Kanzeon, meaning the one who hears the cry of ordinary people and immediately saves them. In the *Wadeigassui*, Bassui referred to Kannon as described in the *Śūramgama Sutra:* "He was a person who for every sound he heard contemplated the mind of the hearer, realizing his own nature." This is clearly the essence of Bassui's teaching—hence his reverence for this bodhisattva. Bassui had a shrine to Kannon built in the northern part of the Kōgakuan temple grounds and asked to be buried there. In 1387, on the twentieth day of the second month, Bassui sat erect in zazen posture, turned to his disciples, and said: "Look directly! What is this? Look in this manner and you won't be fooled." He repeated this injunction in a loud voice and died. He was sixty-one years old. In accord with his request, he was buried under the shrine of the bodhisattva Kannon.

Bassui's Zen

Bassui received verification of his enlightenment from Kohō Kakumyō, and in the formal sense, his Dharma lineage is traced to

Kohō's line. He makes no mention of this connection—or any other for that matter—in either the *Wadeigassui* or any of the letters to his disciples. It is important, however, to look into his biography and the records of his meetings with his teachers to grasp his Zen teaching.

Many of the Rinzai teachers Bassui visited, including Kohō, had some connection with the Chinese Zen master Chūhō Myōhon who lived at a hermitage, the Genjūan, in Tenmokuzan. The Japanese followers of this Genjū lineage favored Chūhō's reclusiveness and stressed his blend of Pure Land teaching and Zen. They dissociated themselves from the government supported Gozan monasteries, preferring to live in small mountain hermitages. They were known for their austere lives and strong emphasis on zazen. Their influence on Bassui was evident from his strong attraction to practicing in quiet mountain retreats rather than large monasteries. He showed a liking for the elegant simplicity of the Zen master Jakushitsu, who had studied for a time with Chūhō at Genjūan.

Bassui deepened his understanding through his contact with the great Sōtō Zen master Gasan Jōseki. Bassui's teacher Kohō studied with Gasan's teacher Keizan Jōkin, who was credited with spreading Dōgen's teaching throughout Japan. Since Kohō's teacher Shinchi studied for some time with Dōgen, we see Dōgen's influence through three generations of Bassui's lineage. Like many of the ancient Chinese Zen masters, Bassui sought out teachers without regard to lineage—his only criterion was that the teacher must help him deepen his understanding of Zen. He was critical of many of the students at the temples he visited. He had a great respect for the spirit of Gasan's teaching in which Dōgen's stress on attention and care for every detail in one's life was evident. Under Gasan, the strict monastery regulations modeled after those of the great Zen monasteries in China were fully developed. Though Bassui had respect for the spirit from which these regulations grew, he seemed critical of the way the monks at Gasan's temple reduced them to dogmatic principles.

Bassui was also very critical of another type of monk who was perhaps not an uncommon sight at some of the temples he visited. This was one who, disregarding the correct behavior befitting a monk, acted in an eccentric manner, thinking he was behaving in accord with the spirit of the ancient masters. He might get drunk, act rudely, break the precepts, and think that his unconventional behavior was proof of his freedom from the shackles created by formal practice. Many of these monks may have developed some of their ideas from reading the stories of the ancient masters whose unconventional behavior was for the purpose of teaching others too attached to the conventions of the time. It was probably his contact with these monks that made Bassui so cautious in his approach to kōan training. He warned his disciples about studying the sayings of the old masters before seeing into their own nature. He did, however, say that it was necessary to understand these kōans once the student did see into his own nature. "That's why if beginning practitioners were first to look directly into their inherent nature, they would be able to see into all kōans naturally. You should know that even though you clearly understand your own mind, if you can't penetrate the *watō* (kōan) of the ancients, you still haven't realized enlightenment" *(Wadeigassui).*

To guard against blatant disregard for the monastic regulations, Bassui left thirty-three rules of behavior for the monks at Kōgakuan as part of his dying instructions. The first of these rules forbids the drinking of alcohol at Kōgakuan. It reads as follows: "Not a drop of alcohol is to be brought into this temple. Even though it may be said to be for medicinal purposes, no alcohol of any kind should be consumed. Monks from other temples should not drink any alcohol as long as they stay at this temple." Bassui was quite firm in his con-

demnation of the drinking of alcohol. In the *Wadeigassui,* in response
to a question about the importance of keeping the precepts, he says:
"The drinking of alcohol, of all broken precepts, is the most upsetting to the serenity of the mind." Then he goes on to quote from the
Bonmō Sutra (Sutra of the Brahma's Net): "One who hands another
a glass of alcohol, making him drink it, will be born without hands
in his next five hundred births. How much more so will one who
drinks on his own?" Cautioning against thinking of the precepts as
mere warnings against inappropriate outward behavior, he continues: "The true meaning of the precepts is that one should refrain
not only from drinking alcohol but also from getting drunk on nirvana." Although he found this deeper meaning in all the precepts, he
was strict about keeping these precepts outwardly, too. With this
restriction against alcohol, Bassui went so far as to have a shrine built
at Kōgakuan with a deity called Basshushin: the God of Retribution
for Drinking Alcohol.

   Though Bassui says he does not use expedient means but rather
teaches people to look into their own nature, teaching both layman
and monk alike, he does seem to allow practices that are designed for
people whose understanding of the Way is still quite undeveloped.
This is consistent with his vow to teach people in accord with their
capacity. One such practice was the copying of sutras. In the *Wadeigassui* he defends this practice by saying that it is a way of emptying the
mind. He goes even further when he tells his disciples that if they were
to transfer this practice to the deceased through memorial services, it
would also bring about, for the deceased, the power of seeing into his
own nature.

   In parts of the *Wadeigassui,* we find Bassui using stories based on
myths and superstitions that were prevalent in medieval Japan. His
object, however, seems to have been to get his listeners to live in
accord with the Dharma. The major part of the text, on the other

hand, is very consistent and even contemporary in its message. According to Bassui, all the teachings can be reduced to a single precept: Seeing into one's original nature is Buddhahood.

It is clear now, after looking into Bassui's life and practice, that this approach—focusing on the one who is listening to the Dharma right now—came from Bassui's own experience. His intense questioning started, according to his biographer, at age seven and remained the center of his practice throughout his life. He found partial answers to his questions, but they only led him to deeper questioning. Certainly, this practice was not originated by Bassui. He himself points to other Buddhist sources—the *Śūraṃgama Sutra* and the Record of Lin-chi—as examples of texts that formulate this practice of listening to the listener. And indeed, examples of this teaching are not confined to the Buddhist tradition. Bassui's strength was his ability to return always to this fundamental question.

Bassui, at seven years old, wondered who it was that ate the offerings at his father's memorial service. This reflection led him twenty years later to the question: "Who is the master of talking, walking, and eating?" Still thirty years later, as an enlightened Zen master of Kōgakuan, his final advice to his disciples was: "Look directly! What is this? Look in this manner and you won't be fooled." He gives no particular answer—and indeed he never did in any of the records of his talks. He is asking us to question so completely that the inquiry frees us from any particular answer, allowing us to stay with the question, and hence to be with ourselves each moment.

COMMENTS ON THE TEXTS

The three texts translated here, the complete *Enzanwadeigassui-shū* and parts of the *Kana hōgo (Dharma Talks in Japanese)* and the

Kambun hōgo (Dharma Talks in Chinese), are our main sources of the teaching of Bassui. Together they give us a pretty comprehensive picture of this unique Zen teacher. Rejecting the Buddhist establishment of his time and criticizing the Zen of both the Rinzai and Sōtō schools, he developed an approach that was entirely his own. He shunned the methods of those two main schools of Zen during his lifetime, but his own teaching penetrates to the core of both Rinzai and Sōtō Zen.

In the opening talk in the *Wadeigassui* (Bassui's *Zuimonki*), he responds to a laymen's question about the relevance of the phrase attributed to the first patriarch, Bodhidharma: "A transmission outside the scriptures and not through words."

First, in dharma combat fashion, he shocks the student out of his mechanical mode. Bringing this student into the present moment, he continues to delineate what the phrase, "transmission outside the scriptures and not through words" means. Here is Bassui at his best; his words flow like lyrical poetry. He is poetic, but he is also concise. As with his opening shock therapy, he is turning the student back to his own resources.

> The bird flying, the hare running, the sun rising, the moon
> sinking, the wind blowing, the clouds moving, all things
> which shift and change are due to the spinning of the right
> dharma wheel of their own original nature. They depend nei-
> ther on the teachings of others nor on the power of words.

This act of taking statements that students make as well as phrases from traditional texts and elegantly recasting them into essentialist Zen terms that would resonate with most modern religious minds is, more than anything else, characteristic of Bassui's style of teaching.

Though Bassui uses a kind of verbal acrobatics in order to bring his point home, he makes a clear distinction between living and dead words. This distinction goes back to the record of Tung-shan (? – 990), disciple of the great master Yun-mên. In volume 23 of the *Transmission of the Lamp,* Tung-shan defined two kinds of words: If there is any rational intention manifested in words, then they are dead words; if there is no rational intention manifested in words, then they are living words.[8] In the *Wadeigassui,* Bassui defines living words as those words that turn the student back to the self. In a dialog in part III, in talking about the *wato,* or key line of a kōan, Bassui quotes Hyakujō: "All words and sayings gently turn, returning to the self." And then Bassui goes on to say:

> If you truly perfect enlightenment, realizing in this manner,
> not only will the rare words and wonderful phrases of
> Buddhas and patriarchs become the self, but there will be
> nothing in all creation that, after all, is not the self.

This characteristically Zen way of turning students back to there own resources causes frustration in many students as they look for something to do. Though this impasse may not be negative in terms of spiritual advancement, the inclusion in this book of Bassui's *Kana hōgo* helps us deal with this frustration. In the opening "Sermon" in this text, Bassui clearly delineates in practical terms how we can practice in order to understand the mind he is constantly pointing to. "Sleeping and waking, standing and sitting," he tells us, "profoundly ask yourself, 'What is my own mind?' with an intense yearning to resolve the question." In the *Kana hōgo,* he writes to disciples from all walks of life: laypeople and clergy, men and woman, lords and ordinary people. He instructs them on how to practice zazen and how to understand the mind that is beyond rational thinking.

When, in the *Kana hōgo,* Bassui refers to "constantly praying to Buddhas," and "being under the watchful but friendly eye of heavenly beings," we get a hint of a Bassui that does not always resonate with the modern Zen student. Here we are transported to a world of medieval Japan where spirits and heavenly beings float around watching over us. Though apparently contradictory, Bassui seems to have little difficulty conjuring up devils and hells in an attempt to cajole his students into right practice. His reference to the *Sōgo Sutra* from part II of the *Wadeigassui*—in which a monk Sōgo, on a journey, visits what look like temples and monastery bathhouses to find monks who acted in contradiction to the Dharma being tortured in various horrifying manners—is particularly disturbing to one attracted to Buddhism for its rational nonjudgmental philosophy. It certainly disturbed me when I came across it. It also made me wonder what the minds of the people he was addressing were like.

In the latter part of the fourteenth century, Japan was in the throws of a civil war. There was, at the time Bassui was in charge of Kōgakuan at the end of his life, a ruling family, the Ashikaga, however in most of the provinces around the country, anarchy ruled. Temples, as refuges for the disenfranchised, reflected the mood of the country. In the *Wadeigassui* Bassui describes some of these students and how they misunderstand and misuse the Dharma.

> Then there are the rebels. Calling themselves liberated, they throw away their three types of robes and their begging bowls. They don't wear monk's robes; they put on courtly hats, wear skins of dogs, cats, rabbits and deer. They sing and dance and criticize the Right Law. They pass through this world deceiving laymen and women. If someone were to rebuke them for this behavior, they would refer to the homeless sages like Hotei, Kanzan, and Jittoku...saying they are like these monks, while they never amend their erroneous ways in the least. (part III)

In chaotic times like these, all kinds of characters were found in and out of monasteries. Their presence seems to have made Bassui, a rebel in his own right, a stickler for keeping the precepts. To Bassui, using the Dharma as an excuse to ignore right behavior was an indication of a misunderstanding of religious practice. His strong injunctions against the use of liquor, even for medicinal purposes, shows what a problem liquor was in temples during his time.

Bassui's skepticism of kōan practice—though he clearly did not reject kōans—also seems to have been derived from how they were misused during this period in Zen's history. His objection was to monks who study kōans, have an apparent grasp of their meanings, but haven't really had the proper foundation in zazen, hence:

> ...ignore the laws of cause and effect, and treat the alms they
> receive as unimportant. Eating the five spicy foods and
> drinking liquor, they become wild, abuse the Buddhas and
> the patriarchs, condemn good teachers everywhere, and criti-
> cize things of the past as well as the present...they love to
> talk Zen and wish only to be victorious in Zen combat.

When Bassui asks, "Who is the master?" as he did of himself during his own training, and demands that his students pursue this enquiry to its core, not stopping even at realization, but rather, "...throwing out [realization], returning to the one who realizes..." *(Kana hōgo)*, Bassui is pointing to the nature of the Self, which can be understood when one truly learns the nature of "he" who makes decisions, he who moves the arms and legs.... In the words of Rinzai, "...you must recognize the one who manipulates these reflections. He is the primal source of all the Buddhas and every place is home to which the follower of the Way returns."[9]

In bringing people back to the "master who hears, sees..." Bassui, like Rinzai, is steering students away from the feeling, "I know." I believe Bassui would have been in complete agreement with Keizan's description of Dōgen's conversation with Dōgen's master Rujing in the *Transmission of Light:*

> Therefore it has been said, "When you see, there is not a single thing." Having reached this point, Dōgen expressed it by saying he had shed body and mind. Rujing then acknowledged him saying, "Body and mind shed, shed body and mind." And finally, "Shedding is shed."
>
> Once having reached this state, one will be like a bottomless basket. Like a perforated cup—no matter how much you put into it, it is never filled. Reaching this is called "the bottom falling out of the bucket."[10]

Compare this with Bassui in *Kana hōgo,*

> In the end, understanding through reason will completely disappear and you will forget you own body. Then your previous ideas will cease and the depth of your questioning mind will be sufficient. Your realization will be complete as when the bottom falls out from a barrel and not a drop of water remains.

Bassui, like Dōgen before him, was critical of the kind of kōan training that gave the student a false sense of "having arrived." "You must penetrate your kōan to the very core," he told the Abbess of Shinryuji, adding, "The foundation of every kōan is one's own mind" *(Kana hōgo).* But this core for Bassui, is a barrel that won't hold even a drop of water. That is the "original nature" he stresses. Something fluid, something that holds onto nothing, something that "knows it doesn't know."

This fluidity that comes from deep penetration into the meaning of Dharma is what allowed Bassui to deal with so many varied situations in such a creative fashion. He was a strict disciplinarian as seen in his admonitions in *Kana hōgo* not to let down your guard for a moment during practice—referring to attaining a certain degree of understanding through the practice of zazen:

> However, if you think this degree of realization is true
> enlightenment in which you no longer doubt your under-
> standing of the true nature of reality, you will be making a
> great mistake. It will be like giving up hope of finding gold
> because you discover copper.

He responded to questions about Pure Land Buddhist Sutras with clarity and ingenuity, showing how those teachings like all the Buddhist teachings, in the end, point to the One Mind.

Bassui's longer sermons when treating Pure Land Buddhist subjects contrast with his pithy dharma-combat-like treatment of students' questions about traditional Zen sayings. When a student infers that monks' robes might protect a person who commits "small sins," Bassui's response is a surprising display of shock therapy—invoking images of heretics and demons. Though his warning of karmic retribution seems to contradict his usual nondual "pointing to the One Mind," his overriding purpose, as stated by Bassui in his letter to a monk in Shobo Hermitage, is to save all ordinary people before seeking truth for his own sake. Since we are not told who his audience is, we must assume he speaks differently to different people. So for us, living in this present century, his statement in the *Wadeigassui*, "Dharma is inward realization. Non-dharma consists of formal aspects such as name and form, writings and sayings, and so forth. Whether the attachment is to the inner or outer, it always refers to the 'me,'" clearly resonates, while we are taken aback when he refers to violators of the precepts falling into the deepest hells. But we can't remove any of his responses from their cultural or social underpinnings. Nor can we remove Bassui, himself, from this medieval Japanese environment in which he was raised.

What we can do, as a result of the information from these three texts, is come up with an educated picture of a Zen rebel who refused to be pigeonholed. He questioned who he was from his boyhood. The question led him deeper and deeper until he realized that "all views are delusion." Living alone in hermitages through most of his adult life, he developed a single-minded practice that depended neither on buddhas nor bodhisattvas. In keeping with his vow to save ordinary people, he spent the latter part of his life pointing to a zazen practice of looking into one's true nature. Whether he talked with Pure Land Buddhists who interpreted the sutras literally or Zen practitioners who thought they were above the simple teachings of the scriptures, he pointed to one truth that was crystal clear to him:

> Realize that all form is apparition and stop calculating; kill the Buddha when he appears in your mind and ordinary people when they appear in your mind; destroy the world when it appears and the void when it appears…
>
> Do you wish to penetrate directly and be free? When I am talking like this, many people are listening. Quickly! Look at the one who is listening to this talk. Who is he who is listening right now?" (*Wadeigassui,* part III)

What is the significance of Bassui to the world of contemporary Zen? Bassui, like Dōgen and the Chinese Rinzai master Ta-hui before him, critics of the Zen of their day, was trying to make Zen relevant to his world. To make Zen relevant is to give it life. Though

Dōgen was a severe critic of Ta-hui's teaching, both men found fault with the mechanical way kōans were used. Ta-hui was said to have burned the woodblocks of the *Hekiganroku*, a kōan collection that his teacher Yuan-wu compiled, to show his discontent with the excessive use of kōans. As with most religious practices, kōans lost their true meaning when they became agents of political and social purposes within institutions.

Ta-hui saw kōans as a way to transcend ordinary consciousness by reaching an impasse, "a great doubt" staying with this doubt until a breakthrough to a world where rational thinking doesn't penetrate. Dōgen, on the other hand, used language in a creative and original way to understand the true meaning of kōans, a way beyond our normal boundaries of language.[11] Though in the *Wadeigassui*, and the *Kana hōgo* we find instances of Bassui dealing with these paradoxical sayings of the ancestors in ways similar to Dōgen sometimes and similar to Ta-hui at other times, his most characteristic response is that all these sayings point to one's original nature. In answer to a question about which is preferable, looking in the *watō* or looking into one's own nature, he responds:

> Originally these meaningful expressions were all the same.
> Since one thousand or ten thousand phrases simply become
> the one phrase of one's own nature, one's own nature is the
> foundation of the *watō*. Reach the roots and there is no
> lamenting the branches. (*Wadeigassui,* part III)

The importance of Bassui's insistence on understanding one's own nature before trying to understand the phrases of the ancients is most relevant to students today. This practice does not carry with it any cultural trappings that are a big component of the traditional kōans. Kōans, taken from episodes from the lives of the ancient masters pointing to the nature of ultimate reality, became formalized sayings that justified lineage and transmission. They became a kind of code that helped those in charge of institutions maintain their authority during Bassui's time. Bassui's attempt to bring back some life to this Zen practice was short lived if we are to judge it by the practice of kōan Zen in both Rinzai and Sōtō schools in the centuries that followed. Like Dōgen and his attempt to give life to this unique tradition, Bassui was defeated by the needs of large institutions in an authoritarian society.

If we see his work from the point of view of the record he left behind, writings that influenced the Zen master Hakuin and others as they too hundreds of years after him tried to revive Zen during another period of its decline, and if we see this record as a guide to us in developing a practice of vital Zen today, his contribution is quite significant.

Many Zen groups in the West, including those started by teachers from authoritarian societies, have developed new forms that speak to problems of hierarchy, gender inequality, family practice, and social responsibility. They are trying to create a space where people who are serious about Zen meditation can practice without being required to be formally initiated into any sect or school. This seems to be the direction of American Zen.

Much of what Bassui says in these texts suits this kind of practice. He asks his students to rely on themselves. He tells them to turn to the one who is listening, for he or she is the master. That is not the kind of advice that requires a Buddhist community for its implementation. Nor does it seem any less relevant in the present century than it did in the fourteenth when he was giving that talk. But we can't forget that Bassui is a Buddhist monk and is talking in the fourteenth century.

As we try to understand Bassui's relevance to our world today, we need to look at a broader question: What is the relevance of the ancient teachers to contemporary Zen? That they *are* relevant is clear. But when we take their teachings whole, without sifting out what doesn't make sense in a new context, we usually get into trouble. Much of what Bassui says does make sense. Since he was not involved in the politics of religion to the degree that other Zen teachers were, and since his lineage never had significant power and hence didn't have to sink to the need to distort or water down his teachings in a way that sometimes happened with Dōgen,[12] we have a pretty good sense of his intention. We will inevitably see him through our own cultural glasses, but we can also see something that transcends culture. There is something universal in this unique teaching that has kept it alive until today.

PART I

Outside the Scriptures and Not through Words

A LAYMAN SAID: "Though Zen is said to be transmitted outside the scriptures and not through words, there are many more incidents of monks questioning teachers and inquiring of the Way than in the teaching sects."[1] How can Zen be said to be outside the scriptures? And can reading the records of the old masters and seeing how they dealt with kōans ever be considered outside the realm of words? What is the true meaning of the statement, 'Outside the scriptures, and not through words'?"

The master [Bassui] called to him at once: "Layman!"

He responded immediately: "Yes?"

The master said: "From which teachings did that yes come?"

The layman lowered his head and bowed.

The master then said: "When you decide to come here, you do so by yourself. When you want to ask a question, you do it by yourself. You do not depend on another nor do you use the teachings of the Buddha. This mind which directs the self is the essence of the transmission outside the scriptures and not through words. It is the pure Zen of the Tathāgata. Clever worldly statements, the written word, reason and duty, discrimination and understanding, cannot reach this Zen. One who looks penetratingly into his true self and does not get ensnared in words, nor stained by the teachings of the buddhas and ancestors, one who goes beyond the singular road which advances toward enlightenment and who does not let cleverness become his downfall, will, for the first time, attain the Way.

"This does not necessarily mean that one who studies the scriptures and revels in the words of the buddhas and ancestors is a monk of the teaching sects, and one who lacks knowledge of the scriptures is a monk of Zen—which is independent of the teaching and makes no use of words. This doctrine of nondependence on the scriptures is not a way that was first set up by the buddhas and ancestors. From the beginning everyone is complete and perfect. Buddhas and ordinary people alike are originally the Tathāgata. The movement of a newborn baby's legs and arms is also the splendid work of its original nature. The bird flying, the hare running, the sun rising, the moon sinking, the wind blowing, the clouds moving, all things that shift and change are due to the spinning of the right Dharma wheel of their own original nature, depending neither on the teachings of others nor on the power of words. It is from the spinning of my right Dharma wheel that I am now talking like this, and you are all listening likewise through the splendor of your Buddha-nature. The substance of this Buddha-nature is like a great burning fire. When you realize this, gain and loss, right and wrong, will be destroyed as will your own life functions. Life, death, and nirvana will be yesterday's dream. The countless worlds will be like foam on the sea. The teachings of the buddhas and ancestors will be like a drop of snow over a burning red furnace. Then you will not be restrained by Dharma, nor will you rid yourself of Dharma. You will be like a log thrown into a fire, your whole body ablaze, without being aware of the heat.

"When you have penetrated the truth in this manner and do not stop where practice and enlightenment show their traces, you will be called a Zen practitioner. One who comes into close contact with a Zen master is likened to one entering a burning cave—he dies and is reborn. The cave of ignorance is burned out, giving rise to the great function that goes beyond ordinary standards. It is as though a burning forge were applied to a dull piece of steel converting it instantly into a sacred sword. This is the most important point for a Zen practitioner who meets a master and inquires about the Dharma."

Rinzai's Enlightenment

Rinzai asked Obaku: "What is the unequivocal meaning of the Buddhadharma?" Obaku immediately gave him twenty blows with his staff. Repeating this question three times he received twenty blows each time. Rinzai, skeptical of this treatment, left Obaku and went to Daigu. He asked Daigu: "Having asked Obaku the true meaning of the Buddhadharma on three occasions, I was beaten each time. Am I at fault?"

Daigu responded: "This manner of behavior is due to Obaku's warmhearted kindness. It was done out of tender consideration for you. How can you ask whether or not you were to blame?"

Rinzai, upon hearing these words, had a great awakening and said: "Obaku's Buddhadharma is nothing special."

Daigu, grabbing him by the chest, said: "A moment ago you asked if you were at fault or not, and now you turn around and say the Buddhadharma is nothing special. From what line of teaching did you find this?"

Rinzai then struck him three times under the arm with his fist. Daigu, pushing him aside, said: "Your teacher is Obaku. You are not under my charge."

Well, did the behavior of these two old sages, Obaku and Daigu, amount to intellectual resolutions of words and phrases? Through what teachings did Rinzai's enlightenment come?

Ejō of Nangaku's Enlightenment

THEN THERE WAS THE ZEN MASTER Ejō of Nangaku who excelled in learning the scriptures. Before reaching enlightenment he had an interview with the sixth ancestor, Enō. The sixth ancestor asked: "What is it that comes in this manner?" Ejō could not answer at that time, but carried his doubt with him for eight years. He then came to a realization and went to see the sixth ancestor again. The sixth ancestor said: "What is it that comes in this manner?" Ejō replied: "One word of explanation already misses the mark." The sixth ancestor said: "This is still a disease of the mind." Ejō took leave again, and once more spent eight years with this doubt. Finally, having experienced a great awakening, he returned for an interview with the sixth ancestor.

The master again asked: "What is it that comes in this manner?"

Ejō replied: "It's not that there is no realization, but that it doesn't defile me."

The sixth ancestor immediately accepted this response.

A True Teacher Must Have His Dharma Eye Opened

IF YOU WERE ASKED NOW, "Who is it that comes in this manner?" how would you reply? And if you couldn't reply, how would you avoid a beating from the iron staff of the King of Hades?

If this were something that could be grasped through words and scriptures, why couldn't the learned Nangaku come up with a word to answer the sixth ancestor? If Nangaku, not yet having attained enlightenment, were to answer in his ignorance, using his common sense and knowledge of the teachings, he might not have attained satori. Aside from one who instantly penetrates enlightenment with a one-word response, it is rare to find one in this world who, like Nangaku, has directly experienced enlightenment to its core.

Truly, one who understands Dharma is to be venerated. He is the master who, for the sake of others, and in accord with their various stages of development, points them directly to their own mind. I am not saying that making Nangaku's response your kōan will, in the end, bring about satori.

But there are those who, hearing a word from a teacher, have a great enlightenment in which they lose their body and life. Some, alas, after three to five days resolve their doubts, while others take as much as three to five or even ten to twenty years before resolving their doubts. We tentatively give this period of doubt the name "grappling with one's kōan." Though the words may differ and some may realize enlightenment quickly while others take a long time, when realization comes everyone wakes up to his original nature in its perfection. This realization is not based on words or phrases.

Take for example a warrior shooting arrows at the enemy. Some die on the spot upon being hit, while others suffer from the wound and die a few days later. Though the death of the victim may be quick or slow, the assailant wishes to cut off the roots of life immediately. This is called "pointing directly to your mind and seeing into your own nature is Buddhahood." Cutting the roots of birth and death is what I call destroying the body and losing one's life.

The difference between Zen and the teaching sects is like the difference between one who gets hit by an arrow and dies on the spot and one who sees the incident and stands on the side saying this and that about why the person died. The one who sees directly into his own nature is the Zen man; the one who talks about it is from the teaching sect. It is like one having the knowledge of the hotness of fire and the other diving directly into it, cutting away the roots of his life and his understanding from a human standpoint and becoming one with the fire.

For example, though one may be bright and may have recorded the words of the Zen masters of the Five Schools and Seven Sects,[2] though his words may flow like a swiftly flowing stream, if his own Dharma eye has not been opened he is nothing more than a teacher learned in the sayings of the old masters. This will be of little use to him when dealing with the great matter of life and death. It will be like a picture of rice cakes for a starving body. Three yards of explanation doesn't equal one foot of realization. That is why the buddhas of the three worlds and the historical ancestors all pointed directly to the person's mind to make him realize that seeing into his own nature is Buddhahood. This alone is the transmission of the mind seal. There is no other Dharma.

The Six Perfections Are Seeing
One's Buddha-Nature

S OMEONE ASKED: "The buddhas and ancestors used so many methods and means in their teachings, how can there be nothing outside of seeing into your own nature is Buddhahood? Please elaborate on this."

Bassui responded: "I became a monk in my later years, never learning the sutras. You tell *me* what Dharma there is other than seeing into your own nature is Buddhahood."

Questioner: "According to the sutras, the World-Honored One attained Buddhahood after mastering the Six Perfections. How can this be called seeing into your own nature?"

The master replied: "What are the Six Perfections?"

The questioner said: "They are giving *(dānā)*, keeping the precepts *(śīla)*, patience *(kṣānti)*, effort *(vīrya)*, meditation *(dhyāna)*, and wisdom *(prajñā)*. Giving one's possessions to all without discrimination is called *dānā*. Keeping all the precepts strictly without exception is called *śīla*. Treating animosity and kindness impartially, not getting angry when slandered or beaten, is called *kṣānti*. Moving forward in the performance of good deeds without a break in one's journey and carrying out one's vow to completion is called *vīrya*. Sitting meditation [zazen] is called *dhyāna*. It means sitting in the correct posture in a quiet place and stilling the mind. Learning the sutras and teaching extensively and understanding completely the important aims of the Dharma without any hindrance is called *prajñā*."

Bassui responded: "All of these bring you fortune for which you can secure a life in the world of humans or heavenly creatures. Performing these acts is commendable when compared to the acts of evil people—people with minds that covet, harm others, are immersed in hatred, are lazy, lack faith, are unstable in thought and action and ignorant of the Way—who fall into the three evil paths.[3] But one cannot expect to attain Buddhahood from them. The Six Perfections that the Buddha practiced are themselves the right Dharma of seeing one's Buddha-nature. The true light of one's original nature lights up ten thousand precious qualities and distributes this light equally in all directions to people in accord with their needs. This is called *dāna*. Buddha-nature is pure from the beginning, the master of the six sense organs,[4] yet not stained by the six pollutants.[5] The mind and body of one who realizes this will naturally be in harmony. He will not go out of his way to take the appearance of one keeping the precepts, nor will he generate evil thoughts. This is called *śīla*. Since the constancy of Buddha-nature doesn't make any formal distinction between self and other, one in harmony with this will neither be angered when chastised nor rejoice when revered. This is called *kṣānti*. Buddha-nature is originally possessed of considerable benefit; it brings all merit to its completion, developing myriads of dharmas. It passes into the future, having no limits. This is called *vīrya*. Buddha-nature is unchanging, detached from all phenomena, goes beyond sects, forsakes rules, doesn't distinguish between saints and ordinary people, and is not confined by words or colored by values of good and bad. This is called *dhyāna*. Buddha-nature is clear in itself, lighting up ten thousand human qualities. It is the eyes of saints and ordinary people alike, lighting up the world like the sun and moon. It is the light that sweeps across the past and present—the boundless truth of pure light. This is called *prajñā*.

"The wonder of this true nature of ours is limitless. It is like the great ocean with its waves large and small. The six wondrous functions[6] contained in one attribute of this original nature are called the Six Perfections of the Buddha. Hence one of the old masters said: 'As soon as you understand the Tathāgata's Zen, the ten thousand deeds of the Six Perfections fill your body with tranquility.'"[7]

The Six Supernatural Powers Are
Seeing One's Nature

QUESTIONER: "If one who sees into his inherent nature immediately attains Buddhahood, would he possess the six supernatural powers enjoyed by buddhas?"

Bassui: "Seeing into one's inherent nature is possession of the six supernatural powers."

Questioner: "Seeing into one's inherent nature is *one* of the six supernatural powers. How can you say it is all six?"

Bassui: "Buddha-nature is from the outset master of the six sense organs. To keep the master pure and not to be stained by the six dust-producing senses[8] is called the supernatural powers of the Buddha."

Questioner: "That's not what I heard. As I understand it, the six supernatural powers are clairvoyance, clairaudience, mind-reading, knowing past lives, flying, and the power to stop deluded thoughts. How can one attain the six supernatural powers through this one attribute?"

Bassui: "Why should this limitless wonder of our inherent nature be nothing more than the six supernatural powers? This infinite light shines of its own accord and watches over all. It is nothingness; it is a wonder. It is silent: it illumines. Though forms can be seen, one is not deluded by them. This is clairvoyance. Buddha-nature is pure and unstained. When sounds are heard through the ears, the echo of vibrations is clearly discerned, and yet there is no dependence on discriminating thoughts. This is called clairaudience. When you clearly understand the nature of your own mind, you will realize the oneness of the minds of the buddhas of the three worlds, the ancestors and ordinary people of this world, and heavenly beings of other worlds. This is the power of mind-reading. From the moment you realize your inherent nature, your mind will penetrate through aeons of emptiness that preceded creation through to the endless future. Clear and independent, it will not attach itself to the changing phenomena of life and death, past and future, but will remain constant without any obstructing doubts. This is the power of knowing past lives. When you understand the nature of your own mind, it will thoroughly light up the dark cave of ignorance and the original natural beauty will be manifest. In an instant you will pass through the ten directions without stopping in the blue sky. This is your inherent nature's true power to fly through the air. When you understand the nature of your own mind, delusions will change into wisdom. Because *bodhi* is your original inherent nature, it transcends delusion and enlightenment. You won't exist among saints and sinners and won't be stained by the various phenomena. This is the power to stop deluded thoughts."

The questioner asked: "Theoretically what you say about the six supernatural powers may be so. But if they don't manifest themselves physically, wouldn't they be worthless?"

Bassui: "Buddha-nature is originally equipped with many virtues. The Six Perfections become the practices that form the basis for man's perfection within the body. In what way are they worthless?

"Mokuren (Moggaliputta-tissa), one of the Buddha's ten closest disciples, having attained the first of the supernatural powers, entered hell to see his mother. He could not save her, however, from the pains inflicted in the realm of the hungry spirits. What is the benefit of the physical manifestation of the supernatural?

"Mokuren returned from hell and received a command from the World-Honored One. He summoned the monks who were repenting their sins of the last three-month training period—the fifteenth day of the seventh month—and made offerings to them of the four kinds: food and drink, clothing, bedding, and medicine. After receiving their meal, the congregation of monks recited together: "We pray that the mothers and fathers of seven generations will actively practice in accord with the true meaning of *dhyāna*." In a moment, their voices penetrated to the bottom of hell, instantly destroying the wicked karma that causes birth in the underworld. At once these fallen souls were reborn in heaven. These monks, without moving a foot or exerting effort, with just a single word tore down the Iron-Castled hell, as an arrow hits a target without even separating from the bow. Could this be anything other than the supernatural power derived from seeing into one's original nature?

"Not only was Mokuren unable to save his mother through the physical manifestation of his supernatural power, but he himself had only attained the rank of the two lesser vehicles [enlightening oneself without thoughts of saving others]. In the words of the Buddha: 'Even if it means being born as a dog or a fox, don't settle for attainment of the two lesser vehicles; even if it means spending aeons in hell, don't settle for attainment of the two lesser vehicles.' Hearing these words, Mahākaśyapa's[9] wailing voice shook the ten thousand worlds, while Subhūti,[10] in a daze, threw away his begging bowl. What's more, all great saints similarly wept. From this you should realize that physical manifestations of supernatural powers are given by means of karma, the results of attachment to drugs and charms, the evil deeds of demons and heretics, and the powers of delusion.

"Wise men consider physical manifestations of supernatural powers a karmic hindrance; the ignorant, thinking them desirable, seek after them. These monks from the repentance ceremony who, during their summer training, looked within themselves and saw clearly into their own nature, understanding Dharma, are called monks of *Jishi* [the atonement]. When a recitation issues from those whose activities stem from an empty mind, there will be no one it will not reach. If this were a result of the power of a mantra, why wouldn't Mokuren also know it? It is difficult to measure the extent of the penetration of the power of meditation through ordinary thinking. As the sun shines everywhere in a cloudless sky, how can you place limits on the power derived from seeing into your own nature? The buddhas, numerous as the sands of the Ganges, could not say enough about it. It can collect the great sea on the edge of a hair, place Mount Sumeru in a poppy seed, and fit thirty-two thousand lion-style thrones and eighty thousand monks in a ten-foot-square room, the room being neither too large nor too small. With one bowl of rice, offerings can be made to countless numbers of saints. Yet Dharma is not anything unusual. The words of this ragged monk cannot describe this supernatural power properly. It's like a spinning wheel that moves faster than a flash of lightning. When its full function manifests itself, it cannot be seen even with the eyes of the Buddha. As its activity spreads to all, it destroys the power of evil demons, blows out the burning charcoal under boiling kettles and flaming kilns of hell, and with a shout it smashes the tree of swords and mountain of blades to pieces.[11]

"This power simultaneously gives light and function.[12] It gives the ability to seize or let go in accordance with the situation. When one word is uttered, it sends a sword flying and cuts through a thousand-tracked road. When the wondrous light shines abundantly, it is like the converging of great flames; all within range will lose their lives. Slaying and giving life having their natural order, no corner is left untouched. Behind the southern constellation you bow with folded hands and hide your body in the Big Dipper.[13] Sometimes you are away from your home yet not on the way, sometimes you are on the way yet not far from home.[14] With a shout distinguish between guest and host and cast away the thousand worlds.

"We are all originally in possession of this kind of supernatural power. If you want to understand it, just stop your activity and look within. You will begin to realize it when you penetrate your own nature. All are equipped with this original nature, and each one is perfect. This nature is the master of seeing, hearing, and understanding and is called the Buddha of Great Penetration and Superior Wisdom.

"The immeasurable wondrous activity of this supernatural power is simply based on one's Buddha-nature. What do the four activities [walking, standing, sitting, and lying down] have to do with it?"

The Five Practices of the Lotus Sutra

Someone asked: "What does it mean when it is said in a sutra[15] that if we perform the five practices—receiving and obeying; reading; reciting; expounding; and transcribing this sutra—we will obtain immeasurable merit?"

Bassui answered: "It implies seeing into your own nature and obtaining Buddhahood right now. Receiving and obeying refers to the nature of one's mind. This nature is part of the experience of saints and sinners alike. Each and every one of us is in possession of it in its perfection. Believing and understanding the significance of this nature of one's mind is what is meant by reading and reciting the sutra. Having cut off definitions and explanations and exhausted all thoughts, seeing into one's own nature and becoming enlightened is what is meant by expounding the sutra. Receiving the transmission from one's teacher when one is ripe for realization is what is meant by transcribing the sutra."

The questioner asked: "If, as you say, these five practices are only the one mind and hence not dependent on words, what is the reason for the numerous sutras that resulted from the Buddha's discourses?"

Bassui: "If they didn't exist, how would those attached to form ever learn that there is no Dharma outside of the one mind? For this reason it is stated in a sutra:[16] 'Dhāraṇī (protecting the good and preventing the bad) does not consist of words, but words express dhāraṇī.'"[17]

Questioner: "If the five practices are the same no matter which sutra we choose, why do most people adopt the *Lotus Sutra?*"

Bassui: "The five ideograms that make up the *Lotus Flower Sutra* of the Wonderful Law contain within them the five practices:

Receiving the teaching is expressed in the character Wonderful.

Obeying it is expressed in the character Law.

Reading and reciting it denote the Lotus.

Expounding it is the Flower.

Transcribing it is the Sutra."

Questioner: "How does receive come to mean Wonderful?"

Bassui: "Wonderful is the inherent nature of all people. It is the master of the six senses. This inherent nature receives sensations of all Dharmas, while there is no such thing as a receiver or something that is received. This is the fundamental principle of the character Wonderful. Hence 'receive' comes to mean Wonderful."

Questioner: "Wonderful is as you just stated. How do you equate the meanings of Law and 'obey'?"

Bassui waited a moment and then said: "Have you understood what I just said?"

Questioner: "No, I haven't."

Bassui: "The law as it is always manifests itself; nothing is hidden. All things in nature bear the seal of the one law. All form is interconnected. People obey this law, and the law obeys people. People and the law are one. Hence 'obey' means Law. How do 'reading and reciting' denote the Lotus? When a person aspires to liberation and looks penetratingly into his own nature, the cloud of emotions will disappear, waves of discrimination will cease, and knowledge will become strikingly clear. At this point you should realize that this Wonderful Law is the inherent nature of all buddhas and ordinary beings. It is pure in itself. Though it exists in ignorance and delusion, it is not stained by them. Similarly the lotus living in the mud remains pure in its essence. Hence it is called 'reading and reciting.' The Flower is liberation. This wondrous nature, the heart of original awakening, is said to be beyond ranking and classification. But for a period after a student's first awakening, depending on his ability, there will be shallow as well as deep understanding.

"When, as I said earlier, knowledge becomes strikingly clear and the essence of this reasoning is understood, you have still not entered the realm of true enlightenment. It is only the shadow of reflected light, a guest outside the entrance gate. When knowledge is exhausted, when discriminating views are forgotten, when the lotus of awakening has for the first time been opened, the ten stages of bodhisattvahood can be completed and the two awakenings can be penetrated.[18] Views through Buddha-wisdom will become clear. The buds of the lotus flower will open up and fall away like objects that disappear and appear in the course of being. When students of the Way come this far, they will, for the first time, be fit to discourse on the Buddhadharma and liberate others. For this reason, expounding Dharma is equated to the lotus flower. When this truth is understood, the seal of the ancient buddhas is transmitted to your mind—just as transcribing an old sutra onto a new piece of paper will produce, when completed, the same thing—equating the old with the new. Hence transcribing can be equated with Sutra. Sutra is another name for mind, carrying with it innumerable uncommon meanings.

"From this we can see that these five practices are nothing more than metaphors used as a teaching method. The Buddha used this method to clarify this uniquely precious mind in order to point out to ordinary people that seeing into their own nature is Buddhahood. Ordinary people, who mistakenly seek the Dharma outside their own minds, not knowing that their own selves are the true Buddha, are like deluded children who have forgotten their father. That's why, in seeking to realize the five practices, you will perceive the one mind. Don't covet the leftovers of others while losing the precious jewel that hangs around your own neck."

The questioner then asked: "What is this precious jewel that hangs around one's neck?"

Bassui responded: "When the dragon calls, clouds appear. When the tiger roars, the wind begins to blow."

Transcribing Sutras

Someone asked: "What is the reason for the emphasis, among the five practices, on the rapid transcription of the sutra in a day?"

Bassui responded: "Rapid transcription means sudden enlightenment. How could emphasis not be placed upon it?"

Questioner: "Yes, but formal copying doesn't really have any benefit, does it?"

Bassui: "Since it is linked with seeing into one's original nature, it has some value. How is this so? One who copies a sutra for a day will apply himself completely to the task without relaxing his effort; hence thoughts will not arise and the six sense organs will remain pure. Because the six sense organs remain pure, he will naturally become one with the sutra he is copying. He will at some time approach the state of meditation, and this will be a link to his seeing into his inherent nature.

"If memorial services were performed to transfer the merit of this kind of practice to the deceased, it would be a link to the deceased seeing into his own original nature and attaining Buddhahood. But only when he doesn't create thoughts and is in accord with the teachings of the sutra will the merit reach the deceased. So you should realize that copying sutras and subsequently controlling thoughts and eliminating delusion for a period of time will result in enormous merit within the limits of formal practice. Moreover, if you disregard everything during the twelve daily periods, shutting off all relationships and remaining still while looking into your own nature, there is no reason to doubt you will awaken to the Way. What could compare to this vital path to Buddhahood?"

The True Meaning of Burnt Offerings

S OMEONE ASKED: "It says in the *Lotus Sutra* that one is not a bodhisattva if he doesn't pay homage to the many buddhas with the offering of his burnt body, arms, and fingers. What does this mean?"

Bassui responded: "The burning of body, arms, and fingers symbolizes the eradication of the three kinds of primary illusions: the branches, leaves, and roots.[19] The branches and leaves are the arms and fingers; the root is the body. If you eradicate the three kinds of illusions, you are at that moment a bodhisattva. An ancient master said: 'Through our karma we receive this body, and through this body we again generate karma.' Students of the Way, when you see clearly into your own nature, you will give life to the flow of wisdom; illusionary karmic consciousness will disappear; your mind will empty like the great sky. This is what is meant by destroying the branches and leaves. Then you will cut off views of a pure Dharma body and dissociate yourself from the achievements of rank, while transcending the limits of this Dharma body. This is called consuming the roots.

"If, in this way, you consume the three kinds of illusion, your Buddha-nature will rejoin that of the buddhas in the ten directions, becoming one with them. This is what is referred to as burning your body, arms, and fingers and offering them to the Buddha. If you had burned your physical body and offered it to all the buddhas, what Buddha would receive it?"

The True Meaning of Fasting

S omeone asked: "To the mundane world, fasting is refraining from eating for periods of a week, two weeks, up to one hundred days. Is this a way to Buddhahood?"

Bassui responded: "Fasting does not mean refraining from the formal eating of food. It means refraining from feeding on the roots of delusion. Fasting means looking into your own nature and illuminating your consciousness, cutting off deluded feelings arising from analytical thinking, remaining apart from external phenomena and unattached to the internal void, completely purifying yourself so that things with no more than a thread of meaning become nonexistent in your life. A good teacher of true rank relates to people as a farmer trains his ox, as though he were depriving a starving man of food. If you were mistakenly to take this fasting literally, it would be a case of heresy."

KEEPING THE PRECEPTS

S OMEONE ASKED: "If the essence of all the Buddha's teachings were contained in the practice of looking directly into one's nature and attaining Buddhahood, wouldn't that make the formal practice of keeping the precepts meaningless?"

Bassui responded: "Keeping or violating the precepts is prior to the division of things and ideas (matter and mind)—when essence and form were part of one vehicle. Having not yet seen into his own nature, a person sinks in the sea of passion and discrimination, killing his own Buddha mind. This is the murder of murders. That's why keeping the true precepts is the enlightened way of seeing into your own nature. When deluded thoughts arise, you damage the Dharma treasure, destroy its merit, and hence become a thief. When you give rise to deluded thoughts, you cut off the seeds of Buddhahood and continue the life, death, and rebirth causing karmic activities. This is what is meant by adultery. When you are blinded by deluded thoughts, you forget your precious Dharma body, and, seeing only illusion, you call it your body. This is what is meant by lying. Isolated by deluded thoughts you lose sight of your inherent wisdom and become frantic. This is what is meant by being intoxicated. The other precepts should be understood similarly.

"Thus when your mind is deluded, you are breaking all the precepts, and when you see into your own nature, you are at once keeping all the precepts perfectly. The power from seeing into your own nature will extinguish all delusion and bring life to Buddha-nature. This is the precept not to kill living things. If you put deluded thoughts out of your mind through the power from seeing into your own nature, you will purify the six sense organs and prevent the appearance of the six rebels.[20] This is the precept against stealing. If you see through deluded thoughts by means of this power, the ordinary world will no longer exist. This is the precept against lust. If you see through deluded thoughts by means of this power, you will be able to realize the manifestation of true sublime wisdom. You won't stop at expedient means, mistaking it for the true vehicle, or call the illusive physical body the real one. This is the precept against lying. When you are able to see into your own nature, you will have wisdom. You will not drink the wine of delusion and ignorance. This is the precept against using intoxicants.

"Hence Buddha-nature is the body of the precepts and the precepts are the workings of Buddha-nature. When this body is perfect, its activity lacks nothing. When you desire to mount the platform of the true precepts, you must tread upon the ground of the true self. This is the meaning behind the statement that a young monk having attained Buddhahood need not receive the precepts.

"This is the reason an ancient master said: 'The precept jewel of Buddha-nature leaves its mark on the mind.'[21] Once you have received this precept, it can never be lost. It will not be broken in the boundless future. If you want to uphold this diamond-like unbreakable precept, you must see clearly into your own nature. If you want to clarify your own nature, you must apply the power of meditation wholeheartedly. Abstinence makes this power steadfast and prevents the occurrence of analytical thinking. Both knowledge and ignorance are impure food. Even having the taste of the buddhas and ancestors is still destroying abstinence. True abstinence is the realization of the way of nonthinking. This is called merging completely into the one. Hence it is stated in a sutra:[22] 'Not holding to the conceptual form of the true precepts and having no evil intentions in your mind is called the precept of purity.'

"Of all broken precepts, the drinking of alcohol is the one most upsetting to the mind's serenity. For this reason it is considered a cause of sin. It is said in a sutra:[23] 'One who hands another a glass of alcohol and makes him drink will be born without hands in his next five hundred births. How much more so one who drinks on his own?' So you should refrain from actually drinking alcohol outwardly and transcend life and death inwardly. Nor should you get drunk on the alcohol of nirvana. This is what is called keeping the precept against using intoxicants.

"The breaking and keeping of the precepts penetrates body and mind equally, both externally and internally. This is because there will be no breaking of precepts if you do not let thoughts arise in your mind. And when you break one of the precepts governing the body, thoughts arise. When thoughts arise, various Dharmas are born. When various Dharmas are born, you cannot thoroughly regulate your practice. Without thorough regulation of your practice, it is difficult to clarify your Buddha-nature. Without clarification of your Buddha-nature, you will not escape transmigration through countless births and deaths, and, in the end, you will fall into the deepest pit in hell. Never say that though you break many precepts, diligent practice will prevent your being harmed by it. If this truly has not caused you any harm, why haven't you awakened yet?

"There are two approaches to keeping the precepts. In one, a person while living among laymen, not rejecting delusion, in the midst of evil, internally regulating his practice with care, realizes his own true nature. With the power of *kenshō* [seeing into his own nature] he gradually eliminates deluded feelings and, in the end, purifies the precept jewel and harmonizes the inner and outer—the body and mind. In the other, not being endowed by nature with a sharp intellect, a person doesn't start off practicing with *kenshō* in mind. However, having strong faith, he depends on his aspiration to keep the precepts and gradually purifies his mind within, in the end attaining enlightenment. Although these two approaches— enlightenment through keeping the precepts and harmonizing the precepts through the attainment of enlightenment—are different in principle, they are, after attaining enlightenment, one path.

"The three poisons of greed, anger, and foolishness are the source of the eighty-four thousand delusions. Ignorance is the source of these three poisons. Thus all karmic hindrances are caused by ignorance. We can see from this that ignorance is the source of breaking the precepts. Piling evil deeds on top of the source of karmic hindrances is like burning firewood upon existing fires or piling up rocks and metal on a ship already about to sink into the ocean. How can such a ship ever float under these conditions?

"The precepts are a shortcut for entering the Buddha gate. They are the wall and moat that keep out the six rebels, the fortress that protects the jeweled Dharma. If the fortress is not secure, it will be destroyed by the enemy: life and death. And you will be put to shame before the king of darkness while suffering limitless pain in the lowest chambers of hell. Moreover, the precepts set the standards for this world. When the rules for the Royal Way[24] are followed, there is peace in the four seas. When humanity and justice are disregarded, quarreling will take place. When wind and rain follow their natural order, the country will be calm and peaceful. When the rules for farming are not followed, the five grains will not grow. How much more is this so in the house of the Buddha? Even when, for example, there is no enlightenment, if you earnestly follow the precepts and do not create a great deal of bad karma while doing good deeds, you will have the good fortune to be born in the world of humans or of heavenly beings. It goes without saying that one who outwardly keeps the precepts while inwardly seeking his own true nature will attain the Buddha Way as surely as water combines with water."

The Bodhisattva Jizō

SOMEONE ASKED: "In the sutra of Jizō Bodhisattva it is written: 'The bodhisattva rises early each day and enters various meditations and various hells to free ordinary people from their suffering in the eras without a Buddha.' If these words mean that this is his skillful means for beings immersed in the six realms,²⁵ those who wholeheartedly appeal to this bodhisattva will not fall into evil paths. But why would they seek enlightenment? People would simply appeal for Jizō's guidance. What do you think of this reasoning?"

Bassui responded: "What's your purpose in asking this question?"

"For the sake of understanding the great matter of life and death."

"Then why don't you ask Jizō Bodhisattva?"

"I have only heard his name and seen his picture and statue. I have never seen his real body. How can I ask him?"

"If he can't teach you of the great matter of life and death now, he is not the right teacher for the world today. If he isn't a good teacher for this present world, how can he guide you after you leave it? If this is the case, then the words 'he guides them through this world and the next' are deluded speech. Yet if you say it is deluded speech, you are slandering the sutra. But if you say it is true, it doesn't conform to what you said earlier. How then could you hope to rely on salvation by the bodhisattva? The words of the sutra are unmistakably clear. Error derives from the reader. As the sutra states that he rises early in the morning and enters various meditative states, could anyone be in any of the many hells when Jizō already abides in the state of meditation? If he were in hell, he could not be in a state of meditation. If he were in meditation he could not be in hell. How could he be in various meditative states and various hells at the same time?"

The questioner replied: "I only understand the words from the sutra. The reality behind those words is not clear."

And Bassui said: "Jizō stands for the mind-nature of ordinary people. *Ji* [the character for earth] is the foundation of the mind. *Zō* [the character for storehouse] is the storehouse of Buddha-nature. It is in this Buddha-nature that all the virtue of ordinary people is contained. Hence it is called the storehouse of the Tathāgata. When the mind is deluded, as many ignorant thoughts as sands of the Ganges arise; when enlightened, this mind gives birth to infinite wonderful meanings. Being the source of good and evil, this mind is called earth. The earth gives birth to trees and grasses, hence it is used as an example here. Nature, the place where all the jeweled Dharmas return, is referred to as the storehouse. That is why Jizō (earth-storehouse) is another name for mind-nature. Originally mind and nature are not separate. They were the one center where ordinary people in the six realms observed and perceived, and where they are masters of the six senses. It is here that they were teachers of those in the six realms. Since the four activities (walking, standing, sitting, and lying down) of buddhas and ordinary people throughout the day and night are the wonderful work of this mind-nature, it is referred to in the sutra as 'each day.' As for, 'early morning,' it refers to the period before the distinction between black and white. Early morning means original nature—where there is no division between buddhas and ordinary people.

"Now, hearing the teaching expressed in this way, what is it that is always acting? If you truly understand this, at that instant you are Jizō Bodhisattva. If on the other hand, you do not understand it at all, then Jizō becomes you. Hence the sutra says: 'Good believers in the Dharma: Because the benevolent bodhisattva has a clear and tranquil mind, he is called the Kannon Holding the Jewel of Suchness and Dharma Wheel. Because nothing can obstruct his mind, he is called the Bodhisattva of Universal Compassion. Because his mind is not subject to birth and death, he is called the Bodhisattva of Long Life. Because his mind cannot be destroyed, he is called Bodhisattva of the Storehouse of Earth. Because his mind has no limits, he is called the Great Bodhisattva.[26] Because his mind has no form, he is called the Mahāsattva.[27] If you all believe in this bodhisattva mind and receive it, you will be one with it and never lose it.'

"So you should realize that all the names of the bodhisattvas are just different names for the nature of the mind. As an expedient in the World-Honored One's sermons, he defined things using certain names, and with these names he pointed to the truth. Ordinary people, unaware of this truth, become attached to the names and, in the hope of attaining Buddhahood, seek the Buddha and Dharma outside their minds. It's like cooking sand in the hope of producing rice.

"In ancient times there was a certain bodhisattva who, though he had not yet attained enlightenment, had developed a compassionate mind. He spent his time building bridges across the Yangtze and Yellow rivers and building roads for ordinary people to come and go. To carry on this work he carried earth and mud on his back until he realized that his nature—that is to say, his own Buddha-nature—was itself the earth, and thus he became emancipated. For this reason the World-Honored One named him the Bodhisattva of the Storehouse of Earth.[28] The vast mind of compassion of this bodhisattva was used as a metaphor to show that the true nature of the Dharma body of ordinary people is everywhere and to teach of the many creations that come from it. How can the virtuous work of any bodhisattva be compared to the magnificent perfection of this wonderful Dharma of mind? Ordinary people, being rather dull-witted, delude themselves and mistake these metaphors for facts. When you truly understand your own mind, you will realize for the first time that the sermons of all the buddhas are nothing more than metaphors to point to the minds of ordinary people."

Karmic Affinity for the Way

A QUESTIONER SAID: "Within the teachings it is said that it is easy for one to believe if the karmic relationship with the teacher is right, and it is easy to enter if the karmic connection to the Way is right. Then no matter how hard I practice the *kenshō* road to realization, I could not be expected to reach enlightenment if my past karma were not right. Should I first try to practice a way that would set my karma right?"

Bassui responded: "It is evident that some people have a karmic inclination for the Way and others do not. Even if one were to preach the way of heretics, the way of evil spirits or liberation for oneself only, those who have a karmic affinity with a teacher, even in a previous birth, will believe his teachings and call him a great teacher. On the other hand, even if one were a buddha or an ancestor, without a karmic affinity for a teacher one would neither believe what he says nor want to be near him. Such people would try to go far from where he dwells and slander him. During the time of the Buddha, there were some who slandered him and became disciples of heretics and demons. Whether you follow the right path or the path of heretics depends on your karmic inclination. Those whose karmic inclination led them to heretics learned the way of heretics and, along with their teachers, transmigrated through countless births, eventually ending up in timeless-hell. Those whose karmic inclination led them on the right path ended up realizing their true nature and becoming enlightened. Thus people searching for a master should first clearly discern whether his way is truly the way of the Buddha and also discern the truth or fallacy of his attainment. If the teacher is a person who has definitely understood the great Way, spare neither life nor fortune—go to him and receive his personal teaching. A truly good teacher, when speaking of the Dharma of karmic change, does not destroy people's sight. He points directly to their minds, showing them their true nature and inducing the attainment of Buddhahood.

"When your karmic inclination for the Dharma has manifested itself, it is easy to enter the Way. The teachings of heretics, the way of the lesser vehicle and path of expedient means, are all established as temporary dharmas. Hence there will be those with karmic inclination toward these dharmas and those without such inclination. With the true Dharma, however, there is not a single person who hasn't the karmic inclination toward it. So whether he is a beginner or an old practitioner, layperson or monk, it goes without saying that all who believe wholeheartedly will attain Buddhahood. When talking about this, therefore, we call it the right Dharma, the original face of all buddhas and ordinary people, the master of seeing, hearing, and perceiving. The eighty-four thousand skin pores, the three hundred and eighty joints—the whole body is the Dharma body. What ordinary person does not have karmic inclination for the Way?

"There is no ice or snow apart from water, and the Buddhahood of ordinary people can be likened to snow and ice melting and becoming water. From the beginning nothing has ever been lost. If one says he has no karmic inclination toward the right Dharma and first wants to practice a method to make this karmic connection, it is like a wave in the ocean searching for the ocean, saying it has no karmic inclination toward it and hence must seek out a means of making this connection. Isn't it just like Yajñadatta searching for his head on top of his head, thinking he has lost it?[29] So it is with buddhas and ordinary people. They are like the water and its waves. Though they are not separated by as much as the width of a hair, because of the one mistaken thought—'I am ordinary'—they think that enlightenment is difficult to realize. While this thought becomes deeply set in their minds, a teacher whose level of understanding is no higher than their own comes along and because of his own ignorance says to laypersons that even a teacher like himself finds it difficult to practice Zen—so how on earth can they, laypeople, ever be suited to this practice? He then preaches a fallacious way and creates karma that leads to hell. Therefore, people who preach to others without clearly seeing into their own nature are like the blind leading the blind.

"The way of Zen began without the establishment of any sect. It is simply a religion that points to the one original mind of all buddhas and ordinary people. This mind is nothing other than Buddha-nature. To see this nature is what is meant by religious practice. When you realize your Buddha-nature, wrong relationships will instantly disappear, words will be of no concern, the dust of the Dharma will not stain you. This is what is called Zen. Attaining Zen is becoming a buddha. This real buddha is none other than the heart of all beings, the master of seeing, hearing, and perceiving.

"When one becomes enlightened in this way, body and mind are both Zen. For whom is it easy to obtain? For whom is it difficult to obtain? When a seeker of the Buddha Way hears a sermon of a teacher of false views, he should say to himself, 'A demon has come to pull me down to Hell,' and stay far away from that false teacher. In the *Sutra of Perfect Enlightenment* it is said: 'Though you seek a good friend,[30] if you meet one who teaches false views, you will not attain true enlightenment. This is called the seed of heretical nature and is the fault of the teacher of false views. It should not be blamed on ordinary people.'

"A teacher of false views is one who, not having seen into his own nature, teaches the Dharma of creation and extinction. In a sutra it is said:[31] 'Generally speaking, existing phenomena are all without substance.' Yung-chia said:[32] 'The immediate severing of roots is the seal of the Buddha. I don't like picking up leaves and looking for the branches.' From ancient times up to the present there has not been a single person among men of discernment who has attained Buddhahood without seeing into his inherent nature. Of the seventeen hundred and one beings listed in the *Transmission of the Lamp,* from the seven buddhas[33] to the successive generations of ancestors, all have pointed directly to people's minds, making them see into their own nature solely and thus become buddhas. Moreover, the virtuous priests who followed all taught the transmission of mind through the mind exclusively. There wasn't a single unenlightened person, from ancient times to the present, who didn't bind people when he taught the dharma of existent phenomena. Enlightened beings earnestly point to the Dharma of mind, while the unenlightened, seeking the Buddha outside the mind, wholeheartedly practice the dharma of existent phenomena. These are as different as black and white. Like fire and water they can never mix. Though the Buddha Way is for the purpose of realizing the important matter of cause and effect, when I see how a passing fancy can cause one to believe a teacher of false views, I realize how easily one's karmic inclination can influence one's beliefs. But the karmic inclination people have toward the Buddha Way is far more intimate than their karmic inclination toward an individual. By Dharma I mean Dharma of mind. Can one be without karmic inclination toward one's own mind? Realizing the Buddha mind with your own mind is like the sky realizing the sky. How then will you deal with a teacher of false views who sets up barriers where there are none?"

Distinguishing between a Teacher of False Views and a True Teacher

SOMEONE SAID: "Even though one has the aspiration and practices the Way, if he meets a teacher of false views, he will surely enter the false path. How can he recognize the difference between a teacher of false views and a true teacher?"

Bassui responded: "If a practitioner wishes to distinguish a teacher of false views from a true teacher, he must first look into the true nature of his own mind carefully, and use this power of realization to make the distinction between the two types of teachers. Even then, trying to perceive the great Dharma from one's narrow viewpoint is like a mosquito trying to bite an iron cow. Clearly, one who tries to discriminate between a teacher of false views and a true teacher through his own feelings is like one who tries to light up heaven with the light of a firefly. How can he ever come close to proper discernment?"

The questioner asked: "In that case, many beginning practitioners who believed in teachers of false views would not only spend their lives in vain, they would also receive the retribution of entering the family of evil demons and fall into hell. Isn't there some sign to make them aware of this mistake?"

And Bassui responded: "It is very difficult to teach one who has not yet clearly opened the eye of the Way the difference between the fallacious and the authentic Buddhadharma or a good and a bad teacher. It's like trying to teach the difference between black and white to one who has been blind from birth. Even though one may say he understands the words to some extent, can he really be in complete agreement? If I may venture to say, however, the mind of the Buddha and ancestors has been passed down through the ages, so you should only believe persons who receive the seal of transmission from a good teacher certified in his attainment. The true teacher is one who has seen into his own nature. One who gives sermons while not having seen into his own nature is a false teacher. Though he may have studied the teachings of the Eight Sects,[34] kept the five precepts, sat in meditation for long periods without feeling sleepy, practiced the Way during the six periods,[35] been in the desireless state of purity, and gathered as many followers as the sands of the Ganges, if he has not been properly certified he should not be trusted. If, for example, he has received the seal of transmission from someone, that person's qualifications should be carefully checked.

"The twenty-first ancestor Vasubandhu,[36] also known as Hengyō Zuda, took one meal a day, never lay down, worshiped the Buddha during the six periods, and lived a life of purity without harboring any desires. A great number of people became his followers. The twentieth ancestor, the Venerable Shayata, approached these disciples and asked: 'Hengyō Zuda practices many religious austerities. Will he attain the Buddha Way?' The disciples responded: 'Our teacher is an ardent practitioner; how could he not attain the Way?' The venerable ancestor said: 'Your teacher is far from the Way. Even though he may have practiced austerities for countless ages, they are all the foundations of delusion.' The disciples responded: 'Venerable ancestor, what accumulation of virtuous deeds allows you to slander our teacher?' The venerable ancestor said: 'I neither follow the Way nor depart from it. I neither worship the Buddha nor have contempt for him. I neither sit long hours in meditation nor sit idle. I neither eat just one meal a day nor am I greedy for more. I desire nothing, and that is what I call the Way.'

"When this reply finally reached Hengyō's ears, his undeluded wisdom was awakened and he felt elated and grateful. If the Venerable Vasubandhu had not met the Venerable Shayata, he would have been a mere wild fox,[37] confusing and deluding the masses all his life. You should realize from this that even if one could display ten million virtues, perform rare and miraculous bodily changes and emit beams of light, if he hasn't clearly understood the great Dharma, all these acts would be demons' deeds. Though in society you may have close contact with many evil men, you should never approach this kind of evil teacher. Why? When a student of the Way sees a foolish man commit sinful deeds, he repents all the more for his own evil deeds and will intensify his aspiration to advance in the Way. If, on the other hand, he had close contact with an evil teacher, he would lose sight of his good cause and enter the cave of the evil spirits of heresy, from which it is very difficult to escape.

"A good teacher is one who combines understanding and practice and has no lingering delusions. These lingering delusions are ones that persist as a result of old habits. The Zen master Engo said:[38] 'If he hasn't cut through to full function, attained the great freedom, why live and die with such a one? Why do I say this? Because he has not eliminated lingering delusions of good and bad, right and wrong.' Tōzan said:[39] 'If you want to distinguish between a truly superior person and a false one, there are three kinds of lingering delusions. They are the lingering delusions of opinion, emotion, and speech. With lingering delusions of opinion, one can't separate himself from the domain of the thinking mind and hence falls into the poisonous ocean. With lingering delusions of emotion, one always looks at things from the standpoint of the intellect, becoming narrow-minded and biased. With lingering delusions of speech, one loses sight of the wonderful teaching of the true nature of things and becomes blinded to its true activity. Please consider these three lingering delusions carefully.'

"One who has not yet exhausted these lingering delusions will be stained by the two aspects—existence and emptiness—and will not find freedom anywhere. This is because he will not have penetrated the truth of his own nature. The great master Bodhidharma said: 'In ancient times there was a monk, Zenshō,[40] who could recite the twelve sections of the sutras, yet he still couldn't avoid the fate of the world of transmigration because he didn't realize his own true nature.' And on another occasion he said: 'If an unenlightened fellow is indiscriminately called a buddha, those who call him so will become great sinners. Many ordinary people will be deceived and led to the world of demons. Even if he is able to give sermons on the twelve sections of many sutras, if he doesn't see into his own nature they are all the sermons of demons.' And again: 'Entering water and fire, climbing the Mountain Ringed by Swords, eating only once a day, sitting long hours in meditation and not lying down, are all ways of heretics—the dharma of perpetual change. If you are aware of the nature of spiritual awakening in your activities and movements, you will attain the mind of the buddhas.'[41]

"That is why a man whose clear eye of truth has not been opened will not know the true teacher from the heretic. Though there is only one Dharma, there are shallow and deep realizations. There are distinctions in the traditional teachings in accord with the shallowness and depth of realization. Though he may have self-knowledge, for example, without clarifying the great Dharma he will not be able to rid himself of the profit-seeking mind. When preaching the Dharma, he may look like 'a man of the Way' but in the depth of his mind he can't forget worldly affairs, he is deeply attached to a substantial dharma, he enjoys giving sermons in temples, and he seeks the respect of others. In other words he is denying the law of cause and effect—speaking on the one hand of emptiness, while acting as though there were substantial existence. Paying homage to a supernatural Buddha or Shinto god and praying for miraculous virtue will increase one's karmic connection to hell. Keep far away from this kind of practice. Bodhidharma said: 'He who makes practice and theory one is an ancestral teacher.' Meeting a great master who is certified by a virtuous teacher, has coordinated body and mind, for whom meditation and precepts are equally understood, who forgets both mind and Dharma, who is not moved by praise or blame, who has attained the true Buddha Way, and in whom the gathering of disciples as numerous as the sands does not arouse pride, is as rare as the *udonge* flower, which blossoms only once in three thousand years. You should risk all, even your life, searching for such a teacher."

THE SACRED BONES OF THE BUDDHA

S OMEONE ASKED: "It is said in a sutra that one who has the sacred bones of the World-Honored One will surely become a Buddha. If one in possession of these sacred bones practices the Way, following a good teacher, isn't this so many leaves and branches?"

Bassui responded: "There are none among buddhas and ordinary people who are not in possession of the sacred bones. The body is called the shrine and Buddha-nature is the bones. When you see into your own nature, illuminating and destroying deluded feelings, your body and self-nature are no longer two; the bones and shrine are one. That's why when worshiping the sacred bones of the Buddha we say, 'Sacred bones of the Truth Body, original ground of the Dharma Body, stupa containing the Dharma World,' and so on. The Truth Body is self-nature—that is to say, the whole body of the Tathāgata. It is called the Wondrous Dharma Body. It is called the sacred bones. Hence one who clearly sees this doesn't think of the physical bones of the Buddha as the true sacred bones. Thus in the 'Teacher of the Law' chapter of the *Lotus Sutra* it is said: 'All those who dwell in the vicinity of this sutra should construct a stupa of the seven precious jewels. Make it exceedingly tall and splendidly adorned, but there is no need to enshrine the sacred bones. Why? Because the Tathāgata's whole body is already contained in it.' The essence of this sutra is that the sacred bones are inside the bodies of all people. Thus while one possesses his own true nature with its sacred bones in an undeluded body, not being aware of this, he holds onto the ashes from the bones of another. Carefully guarding sacred bones is in violation of the essence of Buddhism. Hence the World-Honored One likened this case to one who, having a perfect jewel cached in his topknot or his clothing, is himself unaware of this, and thinking himself penniless, turns to others to beg. If you just turn the light inward in self-reflection and become conscious of the sacred bones of your own nature, you will become a buddha while still in this body. This is called embracing the sacred bones and becoming a buddha."

THE SOLE PRACTICE OF ZAZEN

A QUESTIONER SAID: "It is said that one who practices the Way will remove obstructing demons. If one simply practices zazen and doesn't chant sacred words from sutras, by what grace will he remove these obstructions?"

Bassui responded: "A robber does not break into the home of a poor child. The cave of demons and heretics, on the other hand, is rich with human egos and analytical thoughts. Clearly seeing into one's nature is called practice, and the seat that puts an end to analytical thoughts is called zazen. When analytical thoughts are forgotten, views based on knowledge are also forgotten, leaving no trace of ego. The path where heavenly beings fulfill their desire to offer flowers no longer exists.[42] There is no gate through which demons and heretics can secretly enter. What special incantation can compare with this? It is said in a sutra:[43] 'On perceiving that the five *skandhas* (form, feelings, perceptions, impulses, and consciousness) are empty, one is saved from all kinds of pain and misfortune.' That is why the special incantations cannot be compared with diligent practice of zazen. If, while devoting yourself to practice, you have thoughts of gain, and, thinking it will prevent the interference from demons, you recite invocations from sutras, this kind of reasoning will immediately create a demon inside you, attracting demons from the outside, and causing chaos within,[44] like a stinking carcass attracts blowflies. You will quickly lose sight of the seeds of right karma, add to mistaken views, and in the end enter the world of demons and

have to drink molten iron. Though you may say you clearly understand this reasoning, if you don't actually penetrate it to the core, forgetting yourself, there will be nothing you can do to prevent it from
happening. The phoenix bird will stay away if you don't plant
phoenix trees. Ten million incantations can't compare with once
penetrating the Way of no-mind. Does anyone here realize this?
Who is the one who realizes? *Totsu!*"[45]

Dhāraṇī Is the Originally Enlightened True Nature

A QUESTIONER SAID: "In the teachings it is said, 'One glance at a *dhāraṇī* will eradicate millions of aeons of sins, and you will at once become a Buddha.' How do you feel about this point?"

Bassui responded: "This too is the meaning of seeing into your own nature and attaining Buddhahood. *Dhāraṇī* is the originally enlightened true nature with which everyone is endowed. When you realize this, delusions dissolve and this originally enlightened Buddha-nature is perfected. Of this it is said: 'When you see this *dhāraṇī*, you attain Buddhahood.' It is like the saying, 'When the clouds disappear, the sun shines in the ten directions.'"

"What is the teaching of *dhāraṇī* from the standpoint of this body and mind?"

"Each branch of the coral holds up the moon."[46]

"What is the coral?"

"The brightness of the moon extends without limits.[47] Born at the bottom of the great sea, the coral is said to grow up just as trees do above."

PART II

Amida Buddha and the Pure Land

A QUESTIONER SAID TO BASSUI: "It is said in the *Amida Sutra,* 'Beyond ten thousand billion Buddha lands in the western direction there is a world called the Land of Bliss. In that land there exists a Buddha called Amida who is giving Dharma talks at this time.' I have a few doubts concerning these words. For the arhat,[1] there are stages called the four fruits; for the bodhisattva, there are the ten stages of enlightenment and the equivalent awakening and the wonderful awakening.[2] None of these is equal to the wisdom of a buddha. With these stages of enlightenment, the virtue of the bodhisattva can be considerable or slight, his wisdom great or small, his compassion deep or shallow. In the enlightenment of a buddha, however, there should be neither superior nor inferior. That is why it is said in a sutra:[3] 'Only buddhas can really penetrate existence completely.' Now why did Amida Buddha think it necessary for us to be reborn in the Western Pure Land without stopping in any of the other ten thousand billion Buddha lands? Is there superior and inferior with regard to buddhas also?

"Moreover, if it is west of here, will people still farther west of Amida's Pure Land refer to it as the Eastern Pure Land? And will it be the Northern Pure Land to those in lands to its south? If it is the western direction for people in the ten directions,[4] shouldn't it be an expedient name used for a teaching principle rather than a fixed place? If those in the southern, western, and northern directions are ignored, Amida's vow of salvation will not be universal.

"Again, it is said in the *Amida Sutra:* 'Karmic inclination toward virtue and minor good deeds will not enable one to be born in the Pure Land. If, however, one's mind remains undisturbed for one, two, three, four, five, six, or seven days, when it is time to die, then Amida Buddha, accompanied by various sages, will appear before him. He who is not agitated at the thought of death will instantly be born in Amida's Pure Land.' According to this statement it seems that those who have karmic inclination toward virtue and minor good deeds and whose minds are scattered cannot be born in the Pure Land. But being born in the Pure Land would then depend on the power of the undisturbed mind and not on the power of Amida Buddha. And in the *Sutra of Eternal Life* it says:[5] 'It is impossible for those who slander the Right Law to be born in the Pure Land, even if they recite the invocation to Amida Buddha.' If, as is stated, those who slander the Right Law cannot be born in the Pure Land, it would contradict the vow that says that even those who commit the ten evil deeds and five deadly sins will not be excluded from birth in the Pure Land.[6] How can the Buddhist teachings be in error? I can't comprehend this. What, after all, is the true meaning of this?"

Bassui replied: "I have nothing to say. Even if I were to explain it in detail, people attached to the phenomenal world would not believe me; they would, to the contrary, criticize the sutra. In a sutra it is said[7]: 'Do not preach this sutra among undiscerning people.'"

The questioner said: "It says in the *Sutra of Meditation on Eternal Life*,[8] 'Fools commit many evils and feel no shame. When the end seems near, if they reverently listen to the recitation of the titles of the twelve sections of a Mahāyāna sutra by a good teacher, because they have listened in this manner, the bad karma accumulated over thousands of aeons will be eradicated.' This sutra is one of the three Pure Land Sutras. In light of these words, how can you refuse to explain the lines of this sutra, even to those who are among the very evil?"

And Bassui responded: "If you truly desire to know the meaning, you are not among the very evil. I can't refuse. Western direction stands for the root feelings of ordinary people. Beyond the ten thousand billion Buddha lands is where the ten evil thoughts of ordinary people cease and the ten stages of bodhisattvahood are transcended. Amida means the Buddha-nature of ordinary people. Kannon Bodhisattva, Seishi Bodhisattva,[9] and other sages accompanying Amida Buddha are the wonderful activity of one's self-nature. 'Ordinary people' refers to those with ignorant and deluded minds, minds of analytical knowledge. The time of death refers to the extinction of thought. When the functioning of analytical consciousness is destroyed, feelings are purified; this is referred to as the Pure Land in the West. The deluded mind is referred to as this world. It is said in a sutra:[10] 'If you want to purify the Buddha land, you must first purify your mind; the purity of the Buddha land depends on the purity of your mind.' The cessation of analytical thoughts and the appearance of one's true nature in the original vow are referred to as the appearance of Amida Buddha when the mind remains undisturbed. When you realize your true nature in this way, the eighty thousand delusions will change into eighty thousand wonderful meanings. These are referred to as Kannon Bodhisattva and Seishi Bodhisattva and other sages.

"Thus this place is called the Pure Land in the West but it does not mean that it is a fixed place. Since west is a position controlled by the position of the sun, moon, and stars, the true mind which appears when the mind of analytical knowledge is completely subdued is called the Pure Land in the West. Hence it is said:[11] 'The Buddha land is defined with reference to the truth body; the Buddha body was established with reference to phenomenal objects.' If we take our mind to mean the three Buddha bodies, the Dharma body is Amida Buddha, and the enjoyment body and transformation body are Kannon Bodhisattva and Seishi Bodhisattva. In truth, these are all the One Mind. All pleasure and pain are a result of thoughts of life and death. If you destroy all thoughts, your true nature being no-mind, both pain and pleasure cease. This is what is referred to as the Land of Bliss. Hence the phrase: 'Life and death are already death. Transcending death is the Land of Bliss.'[12]

"By minor good deeds are meant chanting sacred words, reciting sacred names, and formal practices with a mind that seeks gain. It is said in a sutra:[13] 'Wherever particular characteristics may lie, they are all delusion.' If you truly want to know the meaning of being born in the Pure Land, you must first know the master of he who is born in this land. The physical body has never, from its inception, been the true body but, rather, a temporary formation of the five aggregates.[14] After the four elements disperse, what remains to be called the self? If the self is originally empty, what is it that is born in the Pure Land? If there is no master to be born in the Pure Land, what is it that seeks this Land of Bliss? Just extinguish the ever-seeking mind, be rid of thoughts of attachment to form, and the body, consisting of the four elements, will have no individual self. When there is no individual self, the nature of the mind is 'as it is' and there is no aspect of disorder. This is called the Undisturbed One Mind; it is the Straightforward Mind. In a sutra it is said:[15] 'The Straightforward Mind is the abode of the Buddha Way because there is no deception there.'

"Putting aside for the time being what happens after the dissolution of the four elements, what is this master of seeing, hearing, and perceiving that resides in this physical body right now? If we don't even know our own minds, we can't know the truth body of the Buddha. If we don't know this truth body, the demons will appear to us in the form of buddhas and bodhisattvas. When they give off rare fragrance and emit great light, we will inevitably believe in them and be engulfed by the demonic path. If you wish to prevent this error, then, as the Buddha said, for one, two, or seven days you must abandon the ten thousand dharmas and give up the various relationships. Your mind will then become the Undisturbed One Mind. When this happens, deluded thoughts will suddenly cease and the originally awakened mind, the Buddha mind, will appear. Only then will you become aware that the two ideograms *nen* and *butsu* [*Nenbutsu*—"praise to the Buddha"] simply mean the mind is Buddha. This mind sees forms in response to the eyes, hears voices in response to the ears, and speaks through the mouth. This is called the present-day Dharma talk of Amida Buddha. This mind, originally passing through the three worlds (past, present, and future), pervading the ten directions, is the essence of all buddhas and ordinary people. It embraces limitless phenomena, leaving nothing outside its sphere. Even the ten evil deeds and the five deadly sins are originally contained in this mind; it lacks nothing. This is what is meant by the phrase 'the Universal Light embraced by Amida Buddha that excludes no ordinary people.' Hence it is said in a sutra:[16] 'The Buddha body fills the Dharma worlds, appearing before all people everywhere. It moves in response to relationships and in the direction of mental activity, leaving nothing outside its sphere.' The Buddha body already fills the Dharma worlds, so where is there no Buddha land? It equally fills the bodies of all ordinary people. This Buddha body is unchanging truth, clear and wonderful. It is neither Buddha nor ordinary being. Not being limited by names and forms of the many dharmas, it is likened to a lotus flower that grows in the mud and yet is not stained by the muddy water.

"Since the bodhisattva is awakened to the pure untainted mind, he never perceives things as having intrinsic qualities, nor does he perceive things as being devoid of intrinsic qualities. Ordinary people mistakenly become attached to the names of their sects while they reject the essence of the Dharma. Thus, though they say they are practicing the Way, they can't avoid the cycle of birth and death. Or, on the other hand, they may wholeheartedly desire worldly fame and, hence, fall into the three evil paths.[17] The World-Honored One, in response to this, with his power of skillful means said to those seeking after fame: 'The excellence of the Pure Land in the West is wondrous, surpassing any joys of humans and heavenly beings a billion times and prolonging life indefinitely.' A true seeker of the Way, whose mind is not focused on his own fame, would not seek pleasure. Ordinary people who from the beginning have been deeply immersed in seeking fame and are attached to phenomenal existence arouse this kind of pleasure-seeking mind. Knowing this, Shariputra asked the Buddha: 'How can we who seek birth in the Western Land of Bliss, one of the Pure Lands in the ten directions, fulfill this desire?'

"At this time the Buddha answered: 'Karmic inclination toward virtue and minor good deeds will not enable one to be born in the Pure Land. If, however, your mind remains undisturbed for a period of from one to seven days, you will then be born in the Pure Land.'

"This was simply the working of skillful means aimed at helping those who seek fame and profit to turn the light inward. It was designed to put a stop to disorderly thought and to wake up the Buddha mind of one's true self. Thus it is said in the *Lotus Sutra:* 'The Dharma King who destroys existence appears in this world, preaching the Dharma discriminately for all ordinary people according to their needs.'

"If one truly sees into the origin of his own mind, he will forget attachment to phenomenal existence, and his own Buddha-nature will emerge. This is what is meant by the reference to the Buddha as the 'Dharma King who destroys existence.' This is also the meaning of the phrase 'Amida Buddha comes to meet you and lead you to the Pure Land.' When compared with the peace of mind of this kind of awakening, the pleasures of the Western Land of Bliss preached in the sutra do not measure up to one part in a billion. If you become truly awakened in this manner, you will know that the Dharma talks in this sutra are simply baited hooks to catch ordinary people who are sinking in a sea of pain; they are compassionate expedient means for leading them to the Right Law of enlightenment. Thus the sutra says:[18] 'It is impossible for those who slander the right Dharma to be born in the Pure Land even if they recite the *Nenbutsu* and so forth.'

"The Right Law is the Dharma of mind. When you look deeply into your own mind, all attachments to objects—from desiring the Buddhadharma to desiring the worldly dharma—will cease to exist, and there will be no trace of this extinction. Then you will immediately be reborn in the Pure Land. Where will one who slanders the Right Law be reborn? Don't you realize that the *Sutra of Meditation on Eternal Life* points out sixteen images for contemplation?[19] If you ignore these teachings and simply devote all your attention to the genuine desire of being reborn in the Western Land of Bliss, never contemplating your own mind, that grasping thought will become a mind in disorder. This greedy mind will, in its next birth, confront the karma of hell. The birth of this mind brings about the birth of various dharmas. The birth of various dharmas brings about the six states of existence,[20] the four holy states,[21] and the many distinctions. There will be no way then to avoid transmigrating through life and death. When you destroy this mind, you will destroy the various dharmas. When you destroy the various dharmas, all will be empty, concepts of before and after and time will cease to exist, and the Amida Buddha of your original nature will immediately appear before you. He will be everywhere. It is like the appearance of the moon when the clouds disperse.

"One who is enlightened in this way would not be afraid even if, for example, the three evil paths of hell should appear before him;

even if the buddhas came to meet him and lead him to the Pure Land, he would not crave rebirth. Then the many demons would have no way to attack him. If this were truly the case, all of this great earth would be the Buddha body, he would merge with the Buddha, and there would be no thing that has merged. This, in other words, is called the Undisturbed One Mind or the undeluded mind. In a sutra it is said:[22] 'Whoever perceives that all characteristics are in fact no characteristics perceives the Tathāgata.'

"Though there are no shallows or depths in the Buddhadharma itself, there are sudden and gradual insights for those enlightened to the Way in accord with their potential. There are those who have had a great awakening—that is, their eyes have been opened to Buddha knowledge after hearing one word. And there are others who, after progressing from the shallow to the deep, gradually reach higher levels and awaken to Buddha knowledge. Still others progress from the first to tenth stage of bodhisattvahood, advance beyond this point and through the next two stages, the equivalent awakening and the wondrous awakening, and enter Buddhahood. Since Buddhahood is the highest stage of awakening, it is called the Land of Bliss.

"When students of the Way forget thoughts of the ten evil deeds and awaken to their own minds, they don't linger in the ten stages of bodhisattvahood or the two awakenings. They don't involve their minds in views of buddhas or views of Dharma, in the ten-bodied herdsman,[23] or in mastering the occult. Transcending sects and levels of awakening, detached from ability and position, they arrive at the land of the self. This is what is called being born in the Western Pure Land beyond the ten thousand billion Buddha lands.

"In order to teach a portion of the great matter of life and death to highly deluded people, the World-Honored One, with the wisdom of expedient means, borrowed many worldly episodes as examples in his discourses to suit the ability of these people. Though there are ten thousand different examples, in reality they point to the One Mind. When your mind is undisturbed, you are the Buddha as you are. This One Mind is originally undisturbed; it is distinct from aspects of delusion and enlightenment. It is referred to as true thought. The whole body of true thought is called Amida Buddha. If you are attached to the forms that appear in your mind and search for things outside your mind, that is referred to as mistaken thought. Giving birth to a few mistaken thoughts will put you ten thousand billion lands away from the Western Pure Land. Hence the Buddha says in a sutra:[24] 'He who sees me by form, he who seeks me in sound, he walks the way of heresy; for he can't see the Tathāgata.' This Tathāgata is the miracle body, the Dharma body, and so forth. It is the original mind of everyone. Simply stop thoughts that seek this mind elsewhere, return to yourself and look directly, and you will see the Tathāgata. Look! Look! Who is this master that is seeing and hearing right now?"

Awakening Depends Only on Your Aspiration

A QUESTIONER SAID: "Even if one practices the Way, if he doesn't know how to read one word surely he will enter an evil path. Even though he were, for example, to attain enlightenment, without wisdom he could not save people. There are those who say one should practice meditating on mind after studying the sutras. Then there are those who say extensive knowledge and broad studies are the many particles of dust of delusion, which form the seeds of interference to enlightenment. Which of these two statements should I believe?"

Bassui responded: "Enlightenment is one's inherent nature; this inherent nature is Buddha; Buddha is the Way, and the Way is wisdom. Everyone possesses this wisdom; it gives each individual perfect harmony. It is the natural beauty of the true ground and original face of all buddhas and ordinary people. Awakening to this depends only on your aspiration. It makes no difference whether you can read or not. Even if, for example, one cannot remember his own name, and being a man of low intelligence cannot read at all, if he believes this principle he is considered a brilliant man. One of the ancients said:[25] 'The heretics are clever but not wise; they are fools, they are childish ones.' One who sees into his own nature arouses the great wisdom for which there is no teacher, penetrates the ashes of the buddhas and the ancestors, and, in an instant, realizes the principal Dharma teaching of the thousand distinctions and ten thousand divisions, the teachings of the scholars of the Hundred

Houses,[26] and the causes for birth as gods and men. What could be hidden from him? Even if, for example, one studies the teachings of the Eight Sects[27] and the Three Schools,[28] or performs wonderful miracles, compared with the original wisdom it is like a solitary light under the sun—or, worse, like comparing a firefly to the light of the moon."

On the Value of Knowledge

D ID YOU KNOW that Master Tokusan[29] was a great scholar at first? Carrying commentaries on the *Diamond Sutra* when he went on a pilgrimage, he met an old woman on the road selling deep-fried rice cakes. He put down his commentaries and decided to buy some to satisfy his desire for something light to eat.[30] The old woman said to him: "What is that you are carrying?"

Tokusan responded: "Commentaries on the *Diamond Sutra*."

The old woman then said: "I have one question. If you can answer it, I will give you some deep-fried rice cakes as an offering. If you cannot, go and buy them somewhere else."

Tokusan said: "Go ahead and ask."

The old woman then asked: "It says in the *Diamond Sutra* that it is impossible to catch hold of past mind; it is impossible to catch hold of present mind; it is impossible to catch hold of future mind. Revered monk, with which mind will you satisfy your desire for something light to eat?"

Tokusan had no answer. The old woman thereupon mentioned the name Ryūtan, telling Tokusan to visit him. Tokusan went to Ryūtan's temple as he was told, performed the proper salutations, and then left. That evening he went to the master's room and stood there awaiting counsel until night set in. Ryūtan then turned to him and said: "Why don't you leave?"

Tokusan was about to leave when he noticed that it was dark outside. He returned to the master's room and said: "It is dark outside."

Ryūtan took a paper torch and offered it to him. Tokusan was about to take it when Ryūtan blew out the flame. Tokusan suddenly experienced great enlightenment. He then prostrated himself and said: "From this day on I will never doubt the words of all the old masters under heaven." Ryūtan immediately certified his enlightenment. Tokusan then took his commentaries, placed them before the Dharma hall, took a torch in his hand, and held it out saying: "Even the many mysterious teachings I have studied are like a strand of hair in the open sky; even if one masters all the essential knowledge in the world, it is like throwing a drop of water into a great ravine." Then he burned them.

So you see, though this Tokusan was a scholar surpassing others, a man so advanced in letters, still he did not have the power to answer the one question put to him by an old woman selling rice cakes by the side of the road! To the contrary, it was the old woman who had the greater power. Nevertheless, because he met a teacher of right views, it was not difficult for him to become enlightened. If understanding the scriptures could make enlightenment possible, why hadn't he become enlightened before this? And if writings could save people, why would Tokusan have burned the commentaries on the *Diamond Sutra*?

What's more, though the sixth ancestor could not read, it did not interfere with his attaining supreme enlightenment. More than half of the seven hundred monks studying under Obai[31] were learned men. Yet among them not one could equal the sixth ancestor. He received certification in a short time and spread the Right Law to the world from then on. Right up to this day the Five Schools and Seven Sects[32] all trace their lineage to him. Can we say there is no benefit if one doesn't know letters? In ancient times a monk called Zenshō[33] could recite the twelve sections to the sutras, yet he still couldn't see into his own nature. Consequently he slandered the Right Law of the

World-Honored One and fell into the hell of incessant suffering while still alive.[34] Though there were many great teachers in China during the Tang dynasty such as Bodairushi Sanzō[35] and the priest Ruyaku,[36] they did not have the wisdom to understand the true teaching of Bodhidharma. Not believing this true teaching, one of them tried to poison Bodhidharma. How could one of them having even a little power to understand the Right Law ever try to harm Bodhidharma? Reflecting upon this, I feel these people were more ignorant than country folk of today. How could they have ever obtained the enlightened Way? You should realize that wide learning and extensive knowledge for one who has not seen into his own nature are enemies of the Right Law.

On the other hand, if the uneducated were fit for the Buddhadharma, wouldn't every farmer in the country realize it? Thus you should realize that awakening to the Way depends only on one's aspiration and not on whether or not one is educated. When the aspiring heart is shallow, lack of knowledge becomes an obstacle to the ignorant, and knowledge becomes an obstacle to the educated. When the aspiring heart is deep, knowledge becomes the basis for understanding the Way for the learned, and lack of knowledge becomes the basis for understanding the Way for the uneducated. The Way is not a matter of knowing or not knowing. Just abandon everything, return to yourself, and look within. Who is this? Spare no time. It waits for no one.

Know Your Inherent Nature before Studying
the Scriptures

IF YOU DECIDE TO PRACTICE the Way only after studying the scriptures, then the demonic killer, impermanence, will not distinguish between the noble and the common or between the old and the young. If you haven't seen into your own nature and realized the Way, you will have difficulty swallowing even a drop of water.[37] How, then, will you compensate the believers in the ten directions for their alms? If you reach the roots, the branches will not grieve.[38] Isn't it reasonable to start by leaving the myriad things for the moment and, after you clarify your understanding of your inherent nature, pursue learning?

One whose Dharma eye has truly been opened will know the original great wisdom. Why would one then have a strong desire to study? Delicious food has no value to one who has had his fill. Now, if Buddha wisdom is something one yearns for, one should realize that one does not have the Dharma eye. Even if, for example, one were to read a thousand sutras and ten thousand sastras, if the Dharma eye has not been opened, this Buddha wisdom would not be clear. One who has not clearly penetrated Buddha wisdom will not understand even one line of a sutra. The statement, "One is able to read sutras for the first time after one is provided with sutra reading eyes," refers to this. If one views the sayings of the buddhas and the ancestors without the power that comes from seeing into one's own nature, one will interpret the meaning according to their words only and become an enemy of the buddhas past, present, and future. Monks like Zenshō and Budairushi Sanzō are examples of this kind of person. Though one may have, for example, developed bad habits up to now, and be subject to the karma of hell, if he comes to know his inherent nature, he instantly eradicates all kinds of sin just as the kalpa fire[39] completely destroys all the worlds. What obstacles could then remain?

Even Formal Practices Point to the Truth

S OMEONE ASKED: "It is said that when the Little Buddha is imprinted on the void and on the fragrance, one will receive unlimited merit. What does this mean?"

Bassui responded: "The student of the Way arouses a wise thought from his empty mind. This is the activity of the Buddha transformation body, the *nirmanakaya,* within his inherent nature. It is called the Little Buddha. When you turn the light inward, reflecting upon yourself, your analytical mind will return to the void. This is called imprinting the mark of the Little Buddha on the void. As for imprinting the mark of the Little Buddha on the fragrance, fragrance is Buddha-nature. Buddha-nature is the foundation of intelligence. When intelligence is used to see its own foundation, that intelligence loses itself and returns to Buddha-nature. This is called imprinting the mark of the Little Buddha on the fragrance. There is no Dharma outside the mind. Even the temporary formal practices are examples that point to the truth of seeing into your own nature, devised for the edification of ordinary people. Ordinary people misunderstand this, and pursuing these examples, they take them for reality. They delude themselves and become attached to form. This is called heresy. The Little Buddha is imprinted on the fragrance and on the void. If you want to practice this Dharma, you should look into your inherent nature with your own mind. The countless images in the universe are simply the mark of the One Dharma. The One Dharma is the One Mind, the

jeweled precept of Buddha-nature; it is imprinted on the fundamental mind. Do you see that this Buddha-nature imprints itself in
the hearts of all people? The heart is the origin of momentary
thoughts. If you cut yourself off from this Dharma of mind, and the
Little Buddha imprints itself on the fragrance only in the formal
sense, it will be like playing with puppets on a shelf.[40] What merit
is there in this?"

The Meaning of Carving Buddha Images

A QUESTIONER ASKED: "What does it mean when someone carves an image of a stupa or a Buddha and makes rubbings from it daily, calling it religious practice?"

Bassui responded: "This too is seeing into one's own nature. When you realize your own Buddha-nature by yourself, the mind seal will be transmitted. It is like making rubbings of wooden Buddha images. Past and present buddhas are all like this. Mind is transmitted through mind, and nothing more. And the stupa is Buddha-nature. Once one sees into his Buddha-nature, he immediately attains salvation, ultimately escaping the pains of transmigration. It is said in a sutra: "One look at a stupa and you are eternally separated from the three evil paths."[41] If one were to take these teachings from the Buddhist sutras literally, and give discourses on them to others, and if these people were to believe this literal interpretation—that the apparent mark of the Little Buddha is actually imprinted on the fragrance and that they can expect to attain Buddhahood by imprinting images from wooden buddhas on paper—they would think that every look at a stupa would bring them prolonged freedom from evil paths. They would then feel that they need do nothing more than look upon an existing material stupa.

"If, as is written in this sutra, one look upon a stupa will bring prolonged freedom from evil paths, who, birds and beasts as well as humans, would not look upon stupas? And would anyone fall into the three evil paths? If this literal interpretation of the sutra were true, why would anyone be afraid to misbehave? And why would anyone throw away the pleasures of this world to become a monk or a nun, follow the precepts, perform ascetic practices, and search for a good teacher? As for this statement, 'A look at a stupa brings prolonged freedom from the three evil paths,' it means that one who looks directly into his inherent nature will attain prolonged liberation. Never listen to the talk of heretics who say there is a way other than looking into your own true nature."

On Letting Go of Belief in Phenomena

A QUESTIONER SAID: "There is not one among the good teachers from ancient times up to the present who hasn't said that
there is no Buddha existing outside of the mind. Though it is clear
from this that all phenomena are delusion, I am not able to let go of
the belief in the existence of phenomena. Is this a result of lingering
habits from my mind?"

Bassui responded: "You are unable to dismiss lingering habits
simply because you are not looking into your own nature. If you
clearly penetrate this truth of seeing into your own nature, arousing
the great prajñā wisdom and realizing that all names and forms are
illusion, you will never again have feelings of attachment to either
existence or emptiness. Hence it is said in a sutra:[42] 'When you know
it as illusion, you are at that moment separated from it and have no
need for any expedient means.' If you try to remove lingering habits
that come from attachment to form, not yet having seen into your
own nature, you are like one in deep sleep trying to rid himself of a
dream. The desire to rid oneself of a dream is itself a dream. The
knowledge that it is a dream is also nothing but a dream. As for completely waking up from this sleep, no matter how much you seek
something within a dream you will never attain it [in reality]. If you
truly believe in the living Buddha, the Buddha becomes the Dharma
King that destroys existence. The Buddha said:[43] 'All karmic paths
are like dreams, illusions, bubbles, and shadows; they are like a dew-
drop or a flash of lightning—thus shall you think of it.' The Dharma

talks of the living Buddha are like this. If you don't believe these words, even your claim to believe in the living Buddha is based on delusion.

"Bodhidharma is the living ancestor who harmonized the four elements. This old master single-mindedly transmitted the mind seal. He pointed directly to people's minds, showing them that seeing their own nature is Buddhahood. He based his teaching neither on words nor on forms. And though the buddhas of past, present, and future and the historical ancestors all appear in the form of living beings, not one physical body remains; they all perish. Only a word or a phrase remains in this world. Of the words they leave behind, none testifies to the reality of form. They even refute the views of emptiness and nothingness. If it is said that there were buddhas and ancestors who based their teaching on existence, this is completely false. What other kinds of living buddhas and ancestors do you believe in? If you believe in the painted and sculptured images of the ancient buddhas and bodhisattvas, you shouldn't say you believe in living buddhas, but rather that you simply believe in gold, silver, copper, iron, wood, rock, silk paper, modeling clay, and the like. These paintings and sculptured images of buddhas are all the workings of people's minds. Wooden buddhas have never made people. What you have to realize is that mind is the mother and father of all buddhas, and the master of the ten thousand things.

"Though the mind of ordinary people is clear and one with the buddhas and ancestors, unable to believe it you fail to rid yourself of the spirit that attaches to form; therefore you transmigrate through the six realms, binding yourself and enduring pain. Suppose, for example, you were to arouse your aspiration for enlightenment and perform severe ascetic practices. If you desired to harmonize yourself with the path of no-mind while still harboring feelings of attachment to form, it would be like trying to start a fire by striking a rock [with metal] at the bottom of the ocean. Though it is a rock at the bottom of the ocean, if you take it, put it upon land, and then strike it, you will immediately produce a flame. Though every rock is equipped with this nature of fire, as long as it is submerged in water it cannot give rise to flames. All people are equipped with the inclination to spiritual awakening, yet without removing the feeling of attachment to all form, they cannot give rise to this awakening. Do you see why it is said: 'Though Buddha-nature manifests magnificently, those who have feelings of attachment to form cannot see it'? On the other hand, if, interpreting these words incorrectly, you show disrespect for Buddhist images and sutras, you will incur severe punishment. Still, one who forms attachment to them will be a long way too from attaining salvation. If you want to remove all feelings of attachment and attain the way of liberation, you should neither turn to things external, grasping them as 'ordinary' or 'sacred,' nor turn inward and cultivate a center. You should, rather, look carefully into your inherent nature directly; then, for the first time, you will attain it."

The True Meaning of the Four Gifts

A questioner said: "It is essential for me to see into my own nature if I am to attain enlightenment by myself. If I do not recite the sacred invocations from the sutras, however, how am I to give compensation for the four gifts [from heaven and earth, king, teachers, and parents], save the people in the three worlds [of desire, form, and formlessness], and repay the donors from the ten directions?"

Bassui responded: "You should not refrain from reciting the sacred prayers for the deceased.[44] It is a pity, however, when you regard these minor good deeds as truth and don't try to know the way to Buddhahood. You should realize that even a thousand years of reading sutras is not equal to a moment of seeing into your own nature. Before the World-Honored One was enlightened, he sat in meditation for six years in the Snow Mountains [the Himalayas], disregarding the activity of his mind. A bird made its nest on the summit, and reeds sprouted, piercing his thighs, while he sat there looking into his own nature in sitting meditation. At that time what sacred prayers could he have recited? Finally, on the dawn of the eighth day of the twelfth month, he experienced his great enlightenment after which he discoursed on the Dharma to ten thousand people, always in accord with their potential for understanding. He did not recite any sacred prayers. Can it be said, then, that this enlightenment of the Buddha was insufficient to repay the donors in the ten directions? If he had engaged in formal practices like sutra reading exclusively, when would he ever have attained Buddhahood?

All the World-Honored One taught during his life consisted solely of pointing to the One Mind, nothing more. Where his teaching was recorded it came to be called the Sacred Sutras. You have to realize that all the teachings of the sutras make up the table of contents for the Dharma of mind. This table of contents is for the purpose of showing just how important this Dharma treasure is. If you calculate the worth of the table of contents without knowledge of the treasure, it wouldn't even come to half a penny. Even if you do read sutras, it should be because they show that there is no Buddha outside of mind.

"If the World-Honored One hadn't attained enlightenment, he would not have been able to discourse on the Dharma. If he hadn't given discourses on the Dharma, there would be no sacred prayers from the sutras. Names and words for the Buddhadharma—a model for the order of monks, temples, pagodas, and the like—would not have existed either. Would there be any Zen temples referred to as the Five Mountains and the Ten Monasteries?[45] With no temples or pagodas and no teachings from the sutras, how could any beneficial karmic deeds be performed? Without the power of the precepts and effects of good karma, how can people achieve high positions in society and the blessings of the world? Without all the temples and mountain monasteries, where would the official dwellings for monks as well as other institutions upholding the Law of the Dharma be? It is for these reasons that all the buddhas and ancestors, through the power of realizing the One Dhāranī, established the Buddha Way and the Royal Way. Which of these larger temples and mountain monasteries were not established through the power of virtuous deeds and true enlightenment—not to mention the temples so small as to be unknown to most people and so numerous as to be impossible to count in a short time? What's more, the famous temples of the teaching sects all came into existence through the power of the

practice of the great teachers and monks. I have yet to hear of anything ever being established solely through the power that comes
from reading the sacred prayers from the sutras. Even if, by chance,
there are some examples, the effect of the teaching there is shallow
and of no advantage at all. You should realize that all worldly and
Buddhist Dharmas are blessings derived from seeing your true nature
and awakening to the enlightened path. If you don't recognize these
as blessings, how can you understand the reason for repaying the
four favors? Among the four gifts, that of the teacher is considered
paramount. If you clearly understand the meaning of this gift, you
will practice meditating on mind—the most revered truth of our
founder, Shakyamuni Buddha. This is why it is said:[46] 'The instant
severing of the roots is the seal of the Buddha. I don't like gathering
the leaves and searching after the branches.'"

ON RECITING SACRED PRAYERS

O NE WHO RECITES SACRED PRAYERS from the sutras and performs various formal practices but does not have an alert and creative mind may well experience happiness and prosperity in his next life. If, however, his mind remains in this dull state, and he commits evil acts, the crimes he perpetrates may result first in his parents going to hell, whereby his descendant lineage is cut off, and, finally, in his own body sinking into hell. For this reason, this "foolish prosperity" can be called the enemy of past, present, and future. This past, present, and future is referred to as the three worlds. The old master said:[47] "Charity performed for personal reward brings joy of heaven; however, it is like shooting an arrow in the sky—when the momentum is exhausted, it falls." Here is another saying of an ancient teacher: "If one child leaves the world [that is, becomes a monk], nine relatives will be reborn in heaven." A monk is one who leaves the house of delusion; he is a liberated person. A liberated person may not always recite invocations from the sutras and may not perform memorial services; but all those who have contact with him will eventually become believers in the teaching of liberation—how much more so will his nine family members, his mother, father, brother, sister, and so forth. That's why even in the teaching sects the true purpose can be said to be studying the commentaries on the sutras of the sects, contemplating and practicing the teaching put forth in these texts, and attaining Buddhahood. I have yet to hear it reasoned in these sects, much less in the Zen sect, that one can attain the Buddha Way by reciting sacred prayers from the sutras.

On Praising the Buddha's Words

IF THE ATTAINMENT OF BUDDHAHOOD resulted from reading and reciting sutras alone, why would the World-Honored One have sat in meditation for six years? In which records of the Zen sect do you find mention of three periods designated for religious services? Inquiring into it, we find this dates back to the time of the Mongol invasion, during the Kōan era. It was in accord with the wishes of the ruling house then that these services were recited as prayers. This was the first time these services were held. The more I think about it, these three periods of religious service were not prayers but simply the result of a decline in the Buddha Way and the Royal Way. I say this so you won't waste your time on religious services during the three prescribed periods or on worldly literature, but rather, like a monk of true resolve, so you will cut off everything and practice zazen. If you support the path where the teachings are transmitted outside the scriptures, both the Buddha Way and the Royal Way will prosper, and teachers and followers alike will frolic in the great sea of liberation. Then the protection of the many gods will increase, heavenly beings and dragon kings will rejoice, and demons and heretics will all surrender. Can prayer for present and future worlds ever compare with this?

Priest Rinzai said: "You train in the six perfections and the ten thousand practices at the same time. As I see it, they all produce karma. To seek the Buddha and the Dharma is to produce the karma of hell. To seek the bodhisattva way also produces karma. Reading the sutras and commentaries likewise produces karma. The buddhas and ancestors are men who do not search for anything."

If, for example, through devoted practice you do not penetrate to the depth of enlightenment in this lifetime, you will at least have established a link for keeping your human form in future lives, and eventually meet a good teacher and attain enlightenment. Along with this will come the life-sustaining wisdom of buddhas and ancestors, which enables you to save ordinary people. This is what is meant by the reward of Buddha's grace. Which donors would not reap these rewards?

From ancient times up to the present, I have yet to hear of one buddha or ancestor who has been enlightened by reading sacred prayers from the sutras. And though there are those who have realized the Way after hearing the words of the buddhas and the ancestors, it was at a moment when their strong aspiration for seeing into their own nature was ripe, or it was due to the power of their past religious practice. They were people who hear once and have a thousand enlightenments. If the time is right, as a result of their intense aspiration, then their enlightenment can come not only from hearing sutras and commentaries, but from hearing a stone strike a bamboo as did Kyōgen,[48] upon seeing the flowers of a plum tree as did Reiun,[49] or as a result of injuring a foot from stumbling into a rock while crossing a mountain peak as did Gensha.[50] These awakenings all occurred when the time was genuinely ripe for these men to see their true nature. Who would say it was because of the sacred prayers of the sutras? If you want to praise the Mahāyāna Sutras and commentaries and educate people in accordance with them, it is essential to understand this teaching: Mind is Buddha. But without seeing your true nature, you are not able to know the Buddha's wisdom. If you praise the Buddha's words, not knowing Buddha's wisdom, you will misinterpret both and, in spite of good intentions, commit sins.

To Truly Read the Sutras First Open
the Mind That Reads

I N THE *Treatise on the Bright-Eyed Sermon* it is said: "When someone who has not himself awakened to the one true Dharma clings
to such expedient means as provisional teaching in his discourses on
the Dharma, this is called the 'diluted discourse.'" It is also written
in this treatise: "Although there is a time when even those who commit the five deadly sins can liberate themselves, there is no chance for
those who teach the 'diluted discourse.'" What's more, just reciting
part of a sutra with the desire to benefit others is like reciting a recipe
in the hope it will prevent people from starving. It is like a warrior
thinking he will cause the enemies of the court to capitulate by
throwing away his weapons and reciting chapters from the *Tales of
Heike.* This cannot be considered loyalty to the court. If you really
want to repay the donors in the ten directions, look directly into
your own nature, view all three wheels of teaching equally as emptiness, and don't be caught for a moment by any of them. On the
other hand, if you have a mind that seeks gain, repaying donors
would be nothing more than the ignorance of egotism. You would
then be born in the womb of a cow or a donkey in order to pay back
this karmic debt. The three wheels are the donor, the recipient, and
the donation.

If you truly want to read the sutras, you first have to awaken the
mind that reads. All formal readings from the sutras are ultimately
destructive. The wonderful Dharma of one's mind does not change

through successive aeons; it is the essence of all the sutras. If you want to comprehend this essence, you should know that the voices of frogs and worms, the sound of wind and raindrops, all speak the wonderful language of the Dharma, and that birds in flight, swimming fish, floating clouds, and flowing streams all turn the Dharma wheel. When you see the wordless sutra only once, the sutras of all the heavens with their golden words, which fill one's eyes, clearly manifest. If you read the sutras with this kind of understanding, you will never be idle throughout endless aeons. If you do not have this kind of understanding, you will spend your whole life covering the surface of black beans.[51]

Kyōshō[52] asked a monk: "What is that voice outside the gate?" The monk answered: "The voice of a dove." Kyōshō responded: "If you want to avoid the karma of hell, don't slander the true Dharma wheel of the Tathāgata."

"It was clearly the voice of a dove. How could it be the true Dharma wheel of the Tathāgata? If you say it is the voice of a dove, you will slander the true Dharma wheel of the Tathāgata and incur the karma of hell. If you say it is the true Dharma wheel, how is it so? Look at this with your eyes clearly focused.

Again Kyōshō said to a monk: "What is the sound outside the gate?" The monk answered: "The sound of raindrops." Kyōshō responded: "Ordinary people are disordered. They delude themselves and pursue things." The monk asked: "What about you?" Kyōshō answered: "I hardly ever become deluded." The monk asked: "What do you mean you hardly ever become deluded?" Kyōshō answered: "To free oneself from bondage is easy, but the way of freedom is difficult."

Kyōshō was a clear-eyed person. How could he delude himself? If he had not yet been enlightened and had made the statements "I hardly ever become deluded" and "The way of freedom is difficult," he would have fallen into hell. But this was not so. What did he mean by saying "to free oneself from bondage is easy, but the way of freedom is difficult"? Again (in response to Kyōshō's first question), if you say it is the sound of raindrops, you are a disordered ordinary person deluding yourself. If, on the other hand, you seek to express yourself, it is the sound of raindrops. What do you make of this? Even one able to understand this phrase may still only have the eye for the wordless reading of just a few of the sutras. If you haven't attained the way of freedom completely, not even in your wildest dream would you be able to understand what "transmission outside of the teachings" means. It goes without saying that without the eye for the wordless reading of sutras, it would be difficult to consume a drop of water.[53] What of the alms from donors in the ten directions? An ancient master said:[54] "Wordless reading begins when you possess the eye for wordless reading." Monks, laymen, even domestic animals simply cannot avoid alms from donors. Who hasn't received favor from heaven and earth, from the king, from teachers, from parents? The simplest way to pay back these four favors and help those in the three worlds (of desire, form, and formlessness) is not to talk of bright or dull. Just as you are, look and find out: Who at this moment is the master who sees and hears?

Discourses Are Words Pointing to the Mind

A QUESTIONER SAID TO BASSUI: "Like the parable of the rich man in the *Lotus Sutra*,[55] ordinary people delude themselves and search for the Buddha and Dharma outside their own minds. This was so in the example of the rich man's son who ran away from home, leaving his father and breaking off all relations with his family, finally having to beg others for food and clothing.[56] And again, in the 'Universal Gate' chapter it is said: 'If you just think earnestly about the power of Kannon Bodhisattva, you will attain emancipation.' And again: 'When you meet all kinds of misfortune, if you contemplate the power of Kannon even a burning pit will be transformed into a pool.' Still the houses of the believers in Kannon are sometimes burned down, and temples enshrining his image have been burned down too. There are also cases of people contemplating Kannon who meet with misfortune. Looking at things from this point of view, even the words of the World-Honored One become lies.

"In each of the many sutras it says: 'All who receive and obey, read, recite, and copy this sutra will attain Buddhahood.' And with regard to the buddhas and bodhisattvas: 'Each buddha and bodhisattva says there is nothing higher than the recitation of the sutra.' Believers in these various sutras all become arrogant and proud because of this, saying what they believe is the truth and that others' beliefs are inferior. When I see this I wonder whether it is the Buddha who is fooling people, instilling pride in them and sending them to hell, or whether the hearts of ordinary people are wicked. Which is the correct interpretation?"

Bassui responded: "The Tathāgata is he who speaks that which is true, he who speaks that which is fundamental, he who speaks that which is ultimate. He does not speak that which is deceitful, nor does he speak that which is alien.[57] There is no mistake in even one phrase or line of the discourses of the World-Honored One. It is simply that when ordinary people hear a true discourse, because of their ignorance there are a thousand variations and ten thousand distinctions. It's like squinting your eyes to make one moon appear as two. Once you see after clarifying your true nature, all words return to the self like waves by the thousands returning to the sea. It is said in a sutra:[58] 'In the hundred thousand Buddha lands, with the exception of discourses of expedient means, there is only the Dharma of One Vehicle, not a second, nor a third.' This One Vehicle is the One Mind. Those who seek the Buddha and Dharma outside of mind are all children of rich men who have forgotten where their homes are. When you awaken to the unique and wonderful Dharma of your true nature, it is as if the lost child had come home.

"All of you! If you want to return to your homes, simply wake up to your true nature. This mind-nature is the original source of all buddhas. It is the names of all the sutras. Sometimes it is referred to as the Unique and Wonderful Dharma, sometimes as Perfect Awakening, sometimes as Dhāraṇī, sometimes as the Realm, sometimes as the Universe, sometimes as the Pure Land, sometimes as the Dharma World of the Avatamsaka Manifold,[59] sometimes as the Storehouse of the Tathāgata, sometimes as the Eastern Buddha King of Mount Sumeru, sometimes as the Tathāgata of the Land of Fragrance, sometimes as Amida, and sometimes as Yakushi,[60] Fugen,[61] Monju,[62] Kannon, and Jizō. All of these names simply point to the One Mind. Though there are ten thousand different names, there are not even two Dharma realities. For that reason it is written in a sutra:[63] 'The teachings in the sutras are fingers pointing to the moon. When you see the moon yourself, you realize there is no moon to point to after all.' The enlightenment in which you see your true mind and realize your true nature is transmitted outside of the scriptures; it is not based on names and words. That is why it is said: 'When you see the moon, you know there is no moon to point at.'

"If you don't realize that all the discourses of the buddhas and ancestors are words pointing to the mind, you become attached to names and words. Then you belittle others and give rise to personal vanity. What was once medicine becomes poison, and you acquire the karma that leads to hell. It is like the moon shining on a thousand houses. Though a person lecturing on the moon says this moon is the only one, the listener's misinterpretation makes him reason that the moon over *his* house is the only true one, while that over another's house is a false one. Now how could any land in the ten directions have a separate moon? One may say, for example, that ten billion Mount Sumerus have ten billion suns and moons; originally, however, there were not even two. The Dharma of the Buddha's discourses is also like this."

There Is No Buddha or Dharma outside of the One Mind

SINCE THERE IS NO BUDDHA or Dharma outside of the One Mind inherent in all people, in accordance with the student's capacity and the occasion, and when speaking of the nature of ordinary people, if the teacher is lecturing on Amida he will say there is no mind or Dharma outside of Amida. If he is lecturing on the Wonderful Law, he will say there is no Dharma outside the Wonderful Law. If he is lecturing on Kannon, he will say that everything and everyone is Kannon. If he is lecturing on mind, he will say there is no Dharma outside of mind. You should realize that all lectures are given with this intention. Don't you see? Though arhats say there are three poisons,[64] to the Tathāgata there aren't even two kinds of names. Arhats are those who have extinguished eighty-four thousand delusions. But even if there are arhats who still have deluded thoughts, the Tathāgata does not have two kinds of names for them. If you say there are two Dharmas, you slander the Tathāgata. But even though according to this there aren't two Dharmas, there are, depending on the karma of ordinary people, the sharp and the dull, and thus sudden and gradual realizations of the Way, and shallow and deep journeys from delusion to enlightenment. And depending on the depth of the journey, there are lofty and feeble degrees of attainment. Thus it is written in a sutra:[65] "All great sages, despite understanding the formless Dharma, still made distinctions."

Not having attained enlightenment, however, a person holds onto name and form, praising himself and claiming his Dharma to be the One Dharma. He says that certain teachings are to be revered while the rest are inferior. Though insisting on the One at the source, in trying to bring his thoughts into harmony with the One he divides it into two. Though ice and boiling water, for example, were both originally cool water, ice remains hard if it is not melted, and hot water remains hot if not cooled down, and neither can be used in the place of cool water. Or take the example of people tasting the same fragrant tea: If one swallows something foul-smelling, it will interfere with the taste of the tea and he won't be able to smell its fragrance. Whatever the sect, if one clings to its Dharma he will never be in harmony with the Way, not even in his dreams. If you have cataracts in your eyes, flowers seem to fall from the sky in disarray. Hence it is said in a sutra:[66] "If even the Dharma must be discarded, how much more so will that which contradicts the Dharma."

Dharma is inward realization. Non-Dharma consists of formal aspects such as name and form, writings and sayings, and so forth. Whether the attachment is to the inner or outer, it always refers to the self. Again the sutra says:[67] "Give birth to the mind, which has no dwelling place." If one says he is Buddha, he dwells in Buddha; if he says he is an ordinary person, he dwells in the realm of ordinary people. Moreover, from the Zen sect to the Pure Land sect, if you cling to the teaching of any one sect you will dwell in that teaching. When your whole body has no dwelling place, what is this mind? Focus your eyes on this right now. If you truly want to know the scent of tea, you should first purify your mouth so that no other flavor or scent remains there. If you want to realize the Buddhadharma, you must first get rid of the thoughts of one who clings to the Buddhadharma, and instantly return to your original face.

This original face was there before the Buddha appeared in the world, before the occurrence of the One Dharma, before your own birth, when there was nothing to be labeled mind or nature. Only when this original source is given a name, to make it more vivid, do we speak of the power of meditation on Kannon.[68] Thus when you clearly penetrate the nameless, Kannon is you that very instant, and you are Amida that very instant. Then, for the first time, it is proper to say there are not two Dharmas and all are the same, whatever the name. But if, before you have looked into your innermost nature and awakened to the Way, you speak from your own understanding, it is a mistake to proclaim that all sects are different or that there are not two Dharmas.

The Power of Kannon

WHEN THE BUDDHA APPEARED in this world, there lived a certain bodhisattva who practiced after hearing and pondering the teachings, and entered into a deep meditative state. That's why he was given the name Kannon. He was someone who, for every sound he heard, contemplated the mind of the hearer, thereby realizing his true nature. The World-Honored One considered him the highest of the twenty-five perfect bodhisattvas and arhats. This bodhisattva's compassionate mind was exceedingly deep. He applied himself everywhere, giving Dharma talks in accord with the people's capacity, taking great care when instructing ordinary people. Thus the World-Honored One made an example of him, saying that the limitless wonderful activity of each ordinary person's nature is like Kannon's. Actually, no example can approach that which is called the unlimited activity of this mind. Could any bodhisattva ever be like this? Your mind applies itself universally, everywhere. It sees colors with the eyes, hears voices with the ears, smells odors with the nose, forms words with the mouth, grips with the hands, runs with the feet. All buddhas and ordinary people have this blessed power. Each of the ten thousand dharmas was established by this power. Though the clear light of the sun and moon shines everywhere, there are intervals of day and night. With the mind, on the other hand, there is no division of day and night. If you realize this, you are liberated; if you are ignorant of this, you are in danger. The loss of this Dharma treasure and the destruction of this virtue are not unrelated to this deluded mind. The eighty-four thousand delusions have their foundation in your consciousness. This consciousness clings to many forms, increasing the karmic seeds of hell. That is why [clinging] consciousness is the fire of hell. If you see into your true nature, upon forgetting thoughts and imaginings you will turn the karma of ignorance into the great sea of liberation. Hence a sutra says:[69] "Even if you are pushed into a pit of fire, if you focus your mind on the power of Kannon the fire pit will change into earth."

When you see your inherent nature, all delusions of the mind will instantly disappear. That's why it is said that whatever misfortune you meet with, if you contemplate the power of Kannon you will instantly be liberated. If one doesn't believe that this nature is Kannon, seeking him outside of the mind, one becomes the rich man's son who forgets where his home is. If you focus on the finger that points to the moon, calling it the moon, how can this be in harmony with the meaning of the Buddha's teachings? While the World-Honored One was alive he discoursed on the teachings. Many people held onto the names and forms of the part of the teachings they believed in, discussing and measuring the shallowness and depth, the high and low points, of their various beliefs. Before the Buddha appeared in this world, before he spoke even one word, what could be called the Great Vehicle? And what could be called the Small Vehicle?[70] When the World-Honored One's life in this world came to an end he said: "From the period beginning at the Deer Park and ending near the Hiranyarati River[71] with my final nirvana, I didn't preach a single word." With the hammer of the wordless sermon the World-Honored One smashed the sermons he gave during his time of service in the world. It's like giving medicine in response to an illness. After you recover from the illness, the medicine is taken away. To which teachings do these words of the wordless sermon belong? Are they destroyers, are they builders, are they sermons, or are they nonsermons? Let us look carefully into this. When we discuss its shallowness and depth, its high and low points, it is like trying to measure the size of a bird that flew away last night by considering the traces. We are fortunate to have a verse from the World-Honored One composed just before his passing. He said: "I am in possession of the Storehouse of the Eye of the Right Law, the Wonderful Mind of Nirvana, the True Form of the Formless, the Dharma Gate of Subtle Wonder, the Transmission Outside of the Scriptures, which I entrust to Mahākāśyapa."[72] Moreover, this Wonderful Mind is the foundation of all beings. What is this Wonderful Mind of all beings? Carefully focus your eyes and look into this.

The Wordless Sermon

A MONK SAID: "After the World-Honored One smashed the earlier discourses that made use of words, names, and form with the hammer of the wordless sermon, he held up a flower before the huge congregation of a million practitioners with a wink of his eye. The congregation did not know what this meant. Only Mahākāśyapa understood, and smiled. The World-Honored One said: 'I am in possession of the Storehouse of the Eye of the Right Law, the Subtle Mind of Nirvana, and I entrust it to Mahākāśyapa.' In turn Mahākāśyapa passed this Right Law on to Ānanda.[73] It was then passed down through twenty-eight ancestors in the West (India), then on to the sixth ancestor in China, and so on down to the present. Is it correct to say that all the ancestors received the One Dharma from Mahākāśyapa?"

Bassui replied: "Yes it is."

The questioner said: "If that is true, then, when disciples receive the transmission from their teachers, all those teachers should hold up a flower and wink, and all the disciples' faces should break into smiles. Why, then, don't the ancestors, ancient and modern, use the same words to transmit the Dharma?"

And Bassui replied: "You should know that the transmission is not based on words, names, or form."

The questioner then asked: "What about the line, 'I already am in possession of the Storehouse of the Eye of Right Law, the Wonderful Mind of Nirvana; I hand it over to Mahākāśyapa'? Isn't it based on words, names, and form?"

And Bassui said: "Why is transmitting this Wonderful Mind based on words, names, and form? You are like a mad dog beaten by a man and still chasing a lump of clay. Only one who throws away the net after catching the fish and throws away the trap after catching the rabbit is able to understand this."

Finally the questioner asked: "When you say that all buddhas and ancestors transmitted the mind that is beyond names, form, and words, isn't mind a word too? Where can I seek this mind that is beyond words?"

The master [Bassui] immediately called to him: "Revered monk!"

When the monk responded, the master said: "What is this that responds?"

The Meaning of Transmission

A QUESTIONER SAID: "If everyone is endowed with this mind that makes no distinction between buddhas and ordinary people, Mahākāśyapa too should possess it. Why is it said that the World-Honored One transmitted it to him?"

Bassui responded: "This transmission of the One Dharma is not given to begin with. Mahākāśyapa's realization and deep penetration into his own nature, as a result of the direct pointing by the World-Honored One, was confirmed to be the same realization as the Buddha's. If we did not rely on a teacher's certification, there would be those who, not having experienced realization, would nevertheless claim they had, and those who, not having this certification, would claim they possessed it. If these people then delude others who seek the Dharma, they end up destroying the Right Law. With this certification former buddhas could foresee future buddhas, former teachers could recognize future enlightened students. People are not certified at random. People who come to inquire about the teaching are thoroughly scrutinized, and only people with understanding that is in agreement with the Right Law receive certification. This is what is called transmission. The words 'You hear the words, you should understand the teaching; do not judge by your own standards'[74] are for the purpose of understanding this meaning of transmission."

On Monks, Precepts, and Fiery Hells

A MONK SAID TO BASSUI: "One who has not seen into his own nature cannot attain Buddhahood though he may have practiced the conditional dharma[75] for a long time. Nevertheless there are those who say that one who goes through life wearing a monk's robe will not fall into the three evil paths.[76] Is this true?"

Bassui responded: "If you wear a monk's robe, keep your mind in order, uphold the precepts, and never commit even a small offense, it is said that you can avoid transmigration and not fall into one of the four evil realms:[77] the paths of hell, hungry ghosts, beasts, and fighting demons. But if you commit a small offense with regard to body, speech, or mind, how will you avoid the consequences?"

The monk said: "Those who violate the four major prohibitions—murder, stealing, lust, and lying—will, no doubt, fall into the four evil realms. Drinking alcohol is not included among these four prohibitions. Why then do the buddhas and ancestors prohibit it so strongly?"

And Bassui replied: "It's simply because all the prohibitions are violated as a result of drinking alcohol.[78] It is said in a sutra:[79] 'Alcohol is the cause of sin.' If you reflect deeply on this, you will no doubt see that drinking too much alcohol is a great sin."

"I don't doubt that a grave sin will cause a monk great pain. Could you show me proof of a monk falling into hell for committing a small sin?"

The master proceeded to open the pages of the *Sōgo Sutra*[80] and the *Record of My Reflections*[81] and responded: "In the country Shae[82] there were five hundred merchants who had to travel across the great sea on business. They asked the World-Honored One to let the monk Sōgo accompany them as their religious teacher. During their journey, the monk Sōgo lost track of the others near an inn and found himself walking alone. Traveling just a short distance down the road, he could hear the sound of temple bells. Searching in the direction of the bells, he found himself facing a temple. He asked a fellow he met there the reason for the ringing of the temple bells. The fellow said there was a bathing room and people were now entering it. Sōgo, carefully reflecting upon this, said to himself. 'I have come a long way and would like to enter the monks' bathing room.' He then entered the monks' quarters and glanced at the many people inside. They resembled a group of monks. Joining the rest, he entered the bathing room. There he saw bathing accoutrements, bathing clothes, earthen buckets, and long-necked jars all in flames. At that point Sōgo watched as many monks entered the bathroom. When they passed through the entrance, they were burned by fire, their skin and muscles melting away, their bones like burning wicks. Sōgo, horrified, asked these monks: 'Who are you?' The monks responded: 'We are people from Embudai.[83] As our faith in Buddhism is inherently weak, you had better direct your inquiry to the Buddha.' Sōgo, in a panic, ran down the road, leaving the temple behind.

"After only a short distance, he came upon another temple. It was a magnificent temple, beautifully constructed. Once again he heard the ringing of temple bells. Seeing a monk there too, he turned to him and asked: 'What is the reason for ringing the temple bells?' The monk responded: 'The monks will be having their meal.' Sōgo thought to himself. 'Having come a long way, I am extremely hungry and would like to have something to eat.' He then entered the monks' quarters and saw the monks gathered together. The eating utensils, mats, and tablecloths were all in flames; all the people and the room itself were also in flames. It was no different than the previous temple. Sōgo asked them who they were, and they responded like the monks in the previous temple. Sōgo, once again in a panic, left the temple and continued down the road. Not having gotten very far, he again came upon a temple. This temple too, like the previous temple, was having a ceremony of great splendor. Advancing, he entered the monks' quarters and, again, saw many monks. They were sitting on a burning floor scratching and hitting each other, their muscle tissue sticking out through ragged flesh, their bones and internal organs burning like wicks.

"Seeing these monks suffering unbearably in this way, Sōgo returned to where the Buddha was dwelling. Reverently he asked the Buddha the reason why these monks were dwelling in hell.

"The Buddha said to Sōgo: 'What you saw and thought were monks were not monks; what you thought was a bathing room was not. Those people were sinners in hell. They had been monks who left their homes at the time of the Buddha Kāśyapa.[84] They didn't keep the precepts, but rather followed their own ignorant ideas. As it pleased them, they used bathing room accoutrements and other implements belonging to the congregation of monks. Though they were warned by monks who kept the precepts and were told the correct rules of behavior, they paid no attention to the warnings. Since the time of the Buddha Kāśyapa's parinirvana, they have been experiencing the pains of hell and, to this day, have not been able to escape.'

"The Buddha then said to Sōgo: 'What appeared to you as a second temple was not a temple, and the people were not monks. They were people in hell. They left their homes at the time of the Buddha Kāśyapa and didn't practice the five virtues[85] or ring the temple bells to inform the monks when it was time to make use of four types of donation.[86] Instead they quietly made personal use of them. For these acts they have had to sit in pain on a flaming floor until this day.'

"The Buddha then said to Sōgo: 'What appeared to you as a third temple was not a temple, and the people were not monks. They were people in hell. They left their homes at the time of the Buddha Kāśyapa. At that time there were many lazy monks living together. Talking among themselves, they said: "Let us ask a monk who keeps the precepts to practice the Way with us, so we too can attain the true Dharma." They then requested an undefiled Buddhist practitioner to eat, sleep, and practice with them daily. This undefiled practitioner looked for other monks who practiced as he did, and in a while there were many monks practicing the pure Dharma. These monks then pursued the monks who broke the precepts and chased them out of the temple. But those who did not keep the precepts set fire to the temple in the middle of the night, killing many other monks. For these acts they have been made to beat each other relentlessly. They have been suffering this torment since the time of Kāśyapa's parinirvana.

"'Then there was one who planted in the rice fields of the community of monks for his own private use, without giving any of the yield back to the community. When an austere monk admonished him for violating the precepts, saying, "How could you not give of the yield to the community?" he requested the aid of a powerful ruler and disregarded the monks admonishment. He responded to all the monks, saying: "I am not your servant. If you have any strength, why don't you plant for yourselves?" As a result of this act, he was to suffer the pains of hell. Then there was a white-robed fellow[87] who planted crops in the monks' field and didn't give any of the yield to the monks. As a result of this act, he suffered in many ways, having fallen into hell in the form of a field made of flesh.

"'There were communal temple utensils for the monks' daily use. The temple had many donors. A vat of milk was given to the temple, as an offering for immediate communal use, and should have been divided among all the monks. The one who happened to be there to receive it saw that a guest monk was present and hid the vat in the back. After the guest monk left, he divided the milk among the monks. As a result of this act, he was made to suffer in hell in the form of a great flaming vat made of flesh.

"'There was one fellow in charge of administering water to the monks. A certain monk used a little water, returning the rather large amount remaining. Though this fellow in charge should have followed the rule of measuring the prescribed amount, he then began adding up the water returned and no longer distributed this extra water. As a result of this act, he was made to stand in hell in great pain crying, "Water, water!"

"'One fellow blew mucus from his nose right onto the pristine area where the Buddha and the monks were dwelling. As a result of this act, he was made to cut his nose with a sword while burning in hell.

"'A young monk divided the hardened honey among the community of monks. He cut it into pieces and licked the remainder that stuck to the knife. As a result of this act, he had to bear the pain of having his tongue cut into pieces.

"'There was a monk from the high seat[88] who received extra portions of food; he received the portions of one or two other monks besides his own. An austere monk warned that according to the true law the monk in the high seat should not be treated in this manner. The old monk responded to this austere monk, saying: "You understand nothing." Bellowing like a camel, he continued: "Having the position of high seat in this community, I have to recite incantations and give Dharma talks. Sometimes I have to recite devotional songs in Sanskrit, which requires a great deal of effort. Why are you always getting angry and attacking me?" For this action he was given the body of a camel, shouting and wailing as his body burned in hell.

"'Then there was a monk who, relying on the power of a strong lord, acted like a person of saintly virtue, receiving the praise of the four types of disciples (priests, nuns, laymen, and laywomen). He took this praise in silence and, like a saint, he occupied the inherited lecturer's seat, receiving the best food and drink. As a result of this, he was turned into a lecturer's seat made of flesh burning in agony in hell.

"'Then there was one who took the good fruit and flowers from the orchards and fields of the community of monks and made personal use of them or gave them to white-robed people. As a result of this act, he was turned into a flowering tree burning in agony in hell.

"'The two novice monks you saw were not really novice monks. They had been novice monks who left their homes at the time of the Buddha Kāśyapa. They went to sleep embracing each other on a single sleeping mat. As a result of this act, they were made to embrace each other on a sleeping mat while burning in hell, with no relief from this pain up to the present.'

"At this point the World-Honored One said to Sōgo: 'There are many monks in hell, but only a few white-robed ones. Why is this so? Many monks violate the precepts, not following the *vinaya*,[89] mutually deceiving and oppressing each other. They make private use of things belonging to the community of monks. When dividing the food and drink for the community, they do not give equal portions. I tell you, again and again, to make sure you recite the precepts, receive them, and put them into action.' The Buddha then said to Sōgo: 'Like all these wrongdoers who in an earlier life left their homes to become monks and misused the property of the community of monks, thus falling into hell, in the future there will be many white-robed ones who will take property belonging to the community of monks. Their punishment will exceed that of these other monks billions of times, having no bounds. Let me add that if, on the other hand, one gives a contribution to a monk who follows the *vinaya* rules, is a member of the community of monks, follows the path of the true law, ringing the temple bell at the proper time, he will obtain more blessings than words can express. How much more so must this apply to offerings of supplies to the community of monks all around.'"

If You Meditate on Emptiness, You Will
Exhaust Delusion

BASSUI SAID: "Sōgo saw fifty-six levels of karmic activities that sent their perpetrators to hell. The Buddha said that these were all people who had become ordained at the time of the Buddha Kāśyapa. He said they had fallen into hell at the time of Kāśyapa's parinirvana, experiencing pain which continues up to the present. Here [above] I have just presented thirteen cases in summary. With these examples you should be able to surmise the others."

The monk to whom the master [Bassui] had just responded said: "I truly understand the danger of committing these small offenses." He then continued: "According to this sutra there are few laypeople and many monks residing in hell. From this one clearly surmises that these are monks merely in form, who live in temples but break the precepts, straying from the Buddha path. They think they should receive the same benefits as full-fledged monks since they, being monks, are no different. They end up despising and abusing the austere monks. Truthfully, I am one of this former type. How can I avoid the karma of being born in hell? I implore you to show me the means."

Bassui said: "There are no expedient means other than simply looking directly into your inherent nature and stopping the flow of birth and death. One phrase of this sutra says: 'If you perform evil, you will experience hell; if you do good, you will receive the pleasures of heaven; if you meditate on emptiness, you will exhaust delusion and see proof of nirvana.'"

MEDITATING ON EMPTINESS

A NOTHER MONK STEPPED OUT AND SAID: "I have already been able to meditate on emptiness."

Bassui responded: "Tell me how you meditate on emptiness."

The monk said: "During meditation I have complete control over scattered thoughts, and mind and body become one like a clear sky. At this time I have no doubt that my body and mind are originally empty."

Bassui replied: "That's not meditating on emptiness. It's merely the first view of emptiness aroused by all students of the Way. If students arousing this point of view do not meet a good teacher, they will ignore the law of cause and effect and, like an arrow heading for its target, go directly to hell. In meditating on emptiness, you see clearly into your own nature, the five *skandhas*—form, feeling, thought, activity, and consciousness—are all empty, all delusions become extinct, personal views are forgotten, the activity of making distinctions is exhausted, and the various demons have no place to perpetrate their acts. Even with the eyes of a Buddha it cannot be seen, this world of peace and intimacy, this whole reality; it manifests as it is."

Record of My Reflections

A MONK SAID: "Though monks not having the Way-seeking mind cannot practice meditation on the true perception of emptiness, bringing shame to monkhood, they should never cease from practicing single-mindedly. Though some break the precepts, they are actually very few. And if one does happen to break them, he still shouldn't be likened to a layman. What could be the reason so few laymen and so many monks dwell in hell?"

Bassui replied: "The hell-conveying karma that Sōgo questioned the Buddha about was karma from small offenses that caused these people to go to minor hells. Moreover, there were fifty-six grades of offenses, of which I have mentioned only a few in order to summarize the many that Sōgo saw. If I wanted to state the causes for which laymen, including those who committed the ten evil deeds and the five deadly sins, fall into the vast hell, and to include the agonies of hell as a result of the strange karmic obstructions people have in their minds, I wouldn't have the words to describe them. Even if I could, who would believe I was telling the truth? Wise men would know without ever being told, while fools, on the other hand, would laugh at me.

"It is written in *Record of My Reflections:* 'The monk Jikue of Shisōji Temple in Kōryō during the Sung dynasty ate roast meat and was born in the hell of hungry dogs. The Sung monk Hōhō reduced the quantity of food given to the community of monks and became a hungry ghost after he died. The monk Ebin of Sakuji Temple in the province of Eki during the Chou dynasty stole valuables belonging to the community of monks and was reborn as a cow. A Zen teacher took a monk's scant vegetable side dish and was reborn as a servant to the community of monks. The monk Dōmyō of the province of Sō during the Sui dynasty borrowed a bundle of firewood, one of the essential temple belongings, heated up water, and washed his feet, forgetting to repay the debt. After his death, his feet were set aflame for a year. After this time, his roommate, a monk named Gensho, saw an apparition of a temple. Dōmyō, who was at that temple, said to Gensho: "I implore you to buy a hundred bundles of firewood and return them to the monk in charge of essential temple belongings. In addition, copy one section of the *Lotus Sutra*. If you do this, I will escape from my present agony." Gensho acted in accord with the words of Dōmyō, and then turned toward the apparition. But it was hidden, no longer to be seen.'

"This *Record of My Reflections* is a large three-volume book. I have listed five episodes from it. They show the inevitability of the cause and effect relationship. If they hadn't known the great importance of matters like these, why would the ancients have thrown away their lives and fortunes for the Dharma? Even though one may have visited wise men here and there, and sat long periods of zazen without sleep, if he doesn't truly have a mind fearful of birth and death, he would be like a man who finds it difficult to rouse himself to cultivate the land because he is abstaining from the five cereals or like one who cannot endure acupuncture since he feels no immediate pain of illness. With corrupt practice of the Way, you will never manage to penetrate to its depths. You will just give free play to your imagination, increasing your mistaken views, and suffer the agonies of hell.

"If you wish to practice enlightened Zen and open the true Dharma eye, from your first awakening maintain the mind that fears all hells. When this mind penetrates to the marrow and senses the urgency of this matter, there is no self who keeps the precepts; this mind will function in a straightforward manner. Then you will easily disregard worldly feelings and quickly realize the Way of the living ancestors. Think about this carefully."

The Eight Sects and One Mind

A QUESTIONER ASKED: "Is a person who has studied the Eight Sects[90] simultaneously, and has clearly penetrated the One Mind, in error?"

Bassui replied: "The nine-tailed fox yearns for many caves; the golden-tailed lion knows how to change his body."[91]

PART III

On Distinguishing Right Views from Mistaken Ones

A QUESTIONER ASKED: "How do you distinguish right views from mistaken views?"

Bassui: "Whether the perception is right or mistaken will be determined by the heart of the practitioner and not in words or statements. How can it be determined if you do not meet the person directly?"

On Right Paths and Mistaken Paths

THE QUESTIONER CONTINUED: "In that case, if one without disciplined training retires to a mountain for religious practice, he will be making a mistake. Yet in recent times, there have been those who have not received disciplined training from a clear-eyed teacher and have not received certification who retire to a mountain from the time they first aspire to study the Way. After coming down from the mountain in their old age, they succeed in meeting with many people and acquiring reputations as good teachers. Is this improper?"

Bassui responded: "In general, the gathering of many people cannot be equated to the gathering of disciples under the World-Honored One. In the community under the Buddha, the size of the community, large or small, depended on the shallowness or depth of realization of the Way. There are, however, mistaken paths and right paths with regard to Dharma.[1] There are people of great ability and people of little ability. Since these people respond to different elements of the teaching, believing in this aspect or that, it is difficult to decide the true path from the false path by the large number of followers. If one not yet having attained true perception were to gather followers and receive special recognition and consideration, discoursing on the Dharma from his limited perception, he would become a demon and his disciples the hell-dwellers; both would receive the bad fruit thereof. That is why the chances of awakening to the Right Law when you haven't met a teacher with right perception are minutely small.

"Before Gozu[2] became enlightened, stupendous miracles occurred: Tigers and wolves submitted to him, a hundred birds offered him flowers, his retreat was surrounded by a white cloud. When the fourth ancestor went to meet him there and confronted him in Dharma combat,[3] his wild fox cave of many years immediately cracked to pieces and he had a sudden awakening, realizing, for the first time, his previous mistakes. Hence his statement: 'Even the flower offerings of a hundred birds, a shameful scene.' If that old fellow hadn't met the fourth ancestor, he would not have been awakened. He would have remained attached to performing miracles and would have suffered the pain of the infernal regions. Here we can say: Without understanding or awakening, living alone is of no value."

"Before Ma-tsu[4] had penetrated enlightenment, he lived in the mountains practicing sitting meditation for long periods, never lying down. The Zen master Ejō of Nangaku went there and started polishing a tile in front of Baso's retreat, saying he was going to make it into a mirror. He laughed at Ma-tsu for sitting in quiet meditation with the intention of becoming a buddha while not understanding what he, Ejō, was pointing out by his action. As a result of Ejō's laughter, Ma-tsu was immediately enlightened. Had Ejō not gone there and showed this to him, Ma-tsu would have kept sitting in quiet meditation, passing his time in vain.

"From ancient times up to the present, no one who has gone to live alone in the mountains—before having attained enlightenment or having met a teacher of superior ability—has ever passed on the wisdom of the buddhas and ancestors. Though ten million people may gather together, if the source is not deep, the river will not flow for long. That is why all those who aspire to the Way discard mothers, fathers, teachers, and elders, do not consider a thousand *ri* a long distance,[5] are not concerned about hunger or cold, and seek out good teachers. When they come into contact with the teacher, some realize enlightenment after some time, establish a mutual rapport, and leave after receiving verification of their attainment. Others, after a word from the master, begin to understand the import of his message. There are others who, after believing, even to a small degree, put down their walking sticks and place their aspirations right there. Some work tirelessly supervising the running of the monastery; others eat the fruit of trees and wear grass robes; and others eat one meal a day while their lives hang from thin threads.

"Feeling no shame though they are ridiculed and admonished, concentrating on the important matter of life and death, these people let their deluded minds wither, forget their own egos, take no pride in their understanding or attainment, practice rigorously to the point of forgetting the flavor of food, and travel on pilgrimages, forgetting they are walking. They do not collect sayings or phrases of the ancient masters; their true desire is only to meet a teacher. Since their sole intention is the complete understanding of the great matter, they do not limit themselves to thirty or forty years; though their hair turns white and their teeth turn yellow, they do not become idle. When they penetrate directly to the source, even after they receive verification from a good teacher they do not get caught in their own glory or superiority. Some may leave, retiring deep in the mountains, burying their names in a ravine, eating boiled wild roots, nourishing their spirits, not pursuing fame. Others may stay near their teachers and serve them, never seeking the ultimate quiet of sitting idly by themselves.

"I've never heard of anyone who, making this kind of true religious practice his prime objective, did not penetrate the truth. They all promoted this vital wisdom of the buddhas and ancestors. Though they lived in peace and quiet, they could not refrain from appearing in society as a light of direction on a dark road, planting seeds of wisdom in the ten thousand worlds. Aren't these people, in fact, true transmitters of Buddha's grace?"

Bassui said: "How incredible! Today's students of the Way are of inferior character, and their aspiration is superficial. They give no thought to the truth of the great matter of life and death. Though they go to teachers everywhere, they don't want to penetrate completely, all the way to the bottom. They only care about their relation to the teacher and his name, not knowing whether he is a teacher of the Right Law or a heretic. They count names, journey to the east, west, north, and south, and take pride in having met many teachers. Some may, for example, place their faith in one locality, spending a summer in a training session there. During this summer period, however, they just spend their time preparing for their pilgrimage following that training period. Some may consider a place to do a combination summer and winter session, counting the days, and hence making ninety days pass slowly. Others may keep a pouch containing a handwritten chart of the lineage of a Buddhist tradition, wearing it around their necks as proof of their attainment; or they may hold onto sacred relics, putting the related implements in order, secretly forming groups of three to five people, constructing pagodas to put the relics in. They then view these relics together, expressing their strong desire for the most rare and precious among them, and discoursing on the superiority and inferiority of them.

"Some burn their bodies, arms, or fingers, severely inflicting pain upon themselves and getting those who train at the same retreat all worked up, engaging them in useless activities as they themselves neglect their religious practice. Others embrace the gathering of followers, become attached to their lay names, artistic skills, and family names. Still others cannot completely rid themselves of the path of duty. As a result, they lose sight of attentive practice, hold onto their own thoughts and opinions, and indifferently assess the Buddhadharma. Though they try to surpass others with Zen stories and defeat them in question-answer combat, they do not have the power of seeing into their own nature and therefore collect paradoxical words and clever expressions from old masters and keep them in secret, showing them to no one. Using these words and expressions, they write poems and songs and take pleasure in adding their own critical comments to the words of the masters. Through the clever use of words they try to defeat their fellow practitioners. These are all examples of the way of heretics.

"Then there are others who despise the behavior of these kinds of people. They say nothing is necessary other than to simply keep to one kōan. While these people observe people in Zen encounters, their ears are closed. Though they are in the congregations of good teachers, they do not express their own understanding and therefore do not experience true training. Because their nature is such that they can't remove the destructive ideas (literally, 'nails and wedges') that delude them, they concern themselves with one activity around one confined area, and in the end they won't be able to climb out of the hole they have dug for themselves. They keep a few formal precepts strictly, thinking it sufficient if they don't break them. Then they add a number that are, to the contrary, not among the body of precepts usually kept by monks: to refrain from wearing things made of silk or cotton, to refrain from eating salt, vinegar, and the five cereals. Saying they are acting in accord with the teachings of the Buddha, they deceive the sons and daughters of households.

"Others, when they first arouse the mind that seeks the Way, keep the precepts, persevere in zazen, and perform religious practices. When they can keep their thoughts under control for a while, they say they can clearly see their 'original face.' Since this 'original face' has no ego, no being, no Buddha, and no Dharma, 'What,' they say, 'should be called precepts?' They ignore the laws of cause and effect, and treat the alms they receive as unimportant. Eating the five spicy foods and drinking liquor, they become wild, abuse the buddhas and ancestors, condemn good teachers everywhere, and criticize things of the past as well as the present. They shout and chatter at length, joke and laugh, sport in the mountains and at sea, spend the day reciting haughty poems, and admire a refined atmosphere with fine flowers. Meeting others and seeing what they possess, they desire it for themselves. Not caring about their own appearance, or whether they are with laymen or monks, being indifferent to the occasion, they love to talk Zen and wish only to be victorious in Zen combat.

"When these people see others who put an end to their wrong views, realizing their deep-rooted errors, who show true concern when they receive steady alms and treat the precepts as the true Dharma of thusness, who keep their mouths shut, relaxing their wild-horse minds and disregarding their monkey minds as they diligently conduct their religious practice and meticulously apply themselves sitting facing the wall in meditation, they spit, point at these people, and laugh. They say these people are dull-witted and not Zen adepts. They themselves are lacking in courage; their minds are full of pride. They talk of their long practice of Zen while they drag their juniors down the road of heresy. When a good teacher takes them on and tries to influence them to truly practice, they raise their fists, clap their hands, give a shout, and snort derisively. When a good teacher tries to grab hold of them in an attempt to discourage them, they wave their sleeves free and start to dance. They do not so much as turn their heads when they are reprimanded. They truly have an incurable disease; medical care is of no avail. With mistaken views rooted within them, they travel around, critically questioning other Zen students who are no match for them, while their arrogant pride grows. This is what is meant by the saying: 'To embrace the void is to disregard cause and effect. Such confusion and recklessness invite misfortune.'[6] To beginners who have aroused the mind that seeks the Way, I say: Don't ever practice among these people of mistaken views.

"Then there are others whose whole bodies shine with clarity, as the reflection of the moon shines in water, and yet they rest content with this clearly manifest light and consider it the foundation for their inherent nature. This becomes the root of their illusions. And still others ask: If all dharmas are empty, how can one practice? What teaching is there to realize? They say that when you are served tea, just drink it, and when you are served food, just eat it. They sink deeply into a shell of tranquillity, and looking into the *watō* of the ancients,[7] they incorporate them equally into their own view of tranquillity. They reason that all these sayings are without meaning; the ultimate truth, they say, is that mountains are mountains and rivers are rivers. Even in their dreams they have yet to understand the wonder of Buddha-nature.

"Some, not yet having seen into their inherent nature, have heard it said that Buddha-nature is the master of seeing, hearing, and perceiving. When asked about it, they raise their hand, or stamp their foot, and say, 'This is it.' Others, without any understanding, call it the way of no-mind. Or they think that the physical body is like a dream, a vision, or a flower in the void, and the mind is unborn and undying, always existing. Or they understand both body and mind to be illusions, which, after they dissolve into the four elements, return to the void and disappear. Or they consider enlightenment to be the state when one no longer doubts that all form is emptiness, which in the final analysis is the substance of the Dharma body; or they feel that verbal expressions, no matter how few, are all mistaken. They say they will withhold their true experience of enlightenment from even their closest friend. They acquaint themselves with the occult, playing around with spirits. They say that even the clear-eyed do not see what they themselves can see; then they lower their heads and whistle to themselves.

"There are others who eliminate all thoughts making their minds calm and composed. They think that the path of no-mind means that their minds are perfectly clear and cheerful. Still others revel in form to the extreme, love manner and decorum far beyond the behavior of others, and seek the way to gain merit. Or, not having the mind that seeks the Way, others become interested in fame. They desire proof of their attainment from a good teacher, and if they don't receive it, they scornfully denounce the teacher. Or, believing in the law of cause and effect in all situations, some feel that even their failure to realize the Buddha Way is a result of past karma. They say they do not have the karmic connection with the Way and will not become enlightened in this lifetime, while trying to exhaust all bad karma of previous lives by performing various practices of self-abandonment. They make pilgrimages to shrines and temples to gain spiritual merit, recite diverse incantations, count prayer beads, and make hundreds of prostrations, praying for the mind that seeks the Way. These people, in particular, are of extremely low aptitude.

"All these people fear life and death. They are sick in the mind— a sickness that occurs when one seeks the Way while not yet having

developed correct views. Bad as they are, however, they don't compare with those who have no fear of life and death and yet do not
seek the Way.

"Then there are the rebels. Calling themselves liberated, they
throw away their three types of robes and their begging bowls. They
don't wear monk's robes; they put on courtly hats, wear skins of
dogs, cats, rabbits, or deer. They sing and dance and criticize the
Right Law. They pass through this world deceiving laypeople. If
someone were to rebuke them for this behavior, they would refer to
the homeless sages like Hotei, Kanzan, and Jittoku or point to others like Chotō and Kensu,[8] saying they are like these monks, while
they never amend their erroneous ways in the least. Though they
may be similar to these ancients in appearance, in terms of correct
behavior these people are still far from approaching it. Thus it is
written in a text called *The Universal Recommendation on Arousing
the Mind:* 'The priest Chotō was about to eat[9] when, standing
behind him, a blue-faced devil consumed the food and left.'[10]
Whether he be layperson or monk, one who goes near these people
will lose his inclination toward the Right Law and enter the family
of demons. How much more so will these people themselves fall
into hell?

"Even if one were to have all the mistaken views cited here, if he
were to meet a good teacher and realize his mistakes completely, and
if he were to stop these thoughts and penetrate to his inherent nature
as he is at that moment, he would attain the original source of the
path of no-mind and receive the treasure house of the true Dharma
eye—the marvelous mind of nirvana that Shakyamuni transmitted
to Mahākāśyapa. And he could then give medicine to others in
response to their diseases. He could do this on a particularly far-
reaching scale, because having had many diseases himself he would
remember the nature of the medicines used.

"If, on the other hand, a person has not yet reformed and is spending his whole life in vain, when will he ever fend off the iron staff of the King of Hell? Well, is there anybody in this assembly who can escape from these pitfalls—the mistaken views held by the people in the examples I have presented? If there is one who can escape, he should be able to pass through the barriers of the buddhas and ancestors.

What Is the Treasure House of
the True Dharma Eye?

B ASSUI SAID: "The World-Honored One held out a flower with a twinkle in his eye. What was the reason for this? When Mahākāśyapa's face broke into a smile, the World-Honored One said: 'I have the treasure house of the true Dharma eye,[11] the marvelous mind of nirvana. This I pass on to Mahākāśyapa.' Well, all of you, according to your own attainments, what would you call the treasure house of the true Dharma eye? What would you point to as the marvelous mind of nirvana? If you still do not understand, stop saying you have no doubts about Buddhism. Carefully step back and look within, and penetrate into your own selves. What is this treasure house of the true Dharma eye, this marvelous mind of nirvana, that everyone possesses?

"There are those for whom all phenomena totally dissolve: The mind becomes suddenly clear, division between inner and outer no longer exists, everything dissolves perfectly, leaving no borders, and all the worlds in the ten directions are like one round bright jewel with no flaws or shadows. When this world they perceive appears before them, they clap their hands, put on a big grin, and believe they have had a great satori. This is not seeing into their inherent nature. It is no more than an instance when the Dharma-nature appears. Rinzai said: 'The body of Dharma-nature and the ground of Dharma-nature I clearly know to be reflections. Recognize the one who plays with these reflections; he is the primal source of all the buddhas.' If you take these perceptions to be real, it is like seeing a fish's eye as a pearl. When this perceived world manifests, investigate thoroughly right where you are. What is it that is investigating?

"Even though, for example, your wisdom eye opens and you see through both form and emptiness and remain free from agitation and prejudice, you have yet to emerge from the deep pit of attachment to liberation. And even though you penetrate to the nature of truth and deal freely with the kōans passed on by the buddhas and ancestors, having ten answers for every question and a hundred answers for every ten questions—making even a flash of lightning traveling in a mine seem slow in comparison—you are still nothing more than a clever fellow. Not even in your dreams can you understand the path of no-mind.

"An ancient master said:[12] 'The reflection of the moon in a deep lake is not disturbed by the echo from the sound of a bell on a quiet night; and though it appears to remain unscattered when in contact with large and small waves, still it is on the riverbank of life and death.' Another ancient master said:[13] 'The seven hundred monks at Obai's monastery[14] were all men who understood the Buddhist teachings, but this did not become a means of their obtaining the ancestor's robe and bowl. Only the working man Ro,[15] who did not know the Buddhist teachings but understood the path, was able, based on this understanding, to obtain the robe and bowl.'

"A monk asked Nansen: 'How far apart are the Buddhist teachings and the path?' Nansen responded: 'Sand doesn't enter the eyes, water doesn't enter the ears.'[16] So a true man of the Way forgets his views of the Buddha and the teachings and holds to no schemes for passing through the gate. Then the demons and heretics find no path to lie secretly in wait for him. Though he sees with the Buddha eye, he has finally reached a place that cannot be seen, and so he is able to rest for the first time. Gantō Zenkatsu said: 'Keeping aloof from things is superior, chasing after things is inferior.' If you want to transcend the stream of life and death and attain great liberation, separate from external form, do not hold onto opinions within, advance quickly, cutting off your life-root[17] as one would cut his own throat. Return to yourselves and look within; penetrate through to the bottom and confirm this attainment. Spare neither light nor darkness [day nor night]; time waits for no one.

"Even though one may be clear in his understanding of the truth and his commitment to the kind of practice discussed here and has thoroughly investigated it, if he has not yet received confirmation that he has penetrated enlightenment and leaves the vicinity of a good teacher, he will become hindered by his own interpretations and will not be able to comprehend the great matter. Not yet having comprehended the great Dharma, his relationship to the gathering of people under his guidance—merely through his being praiseworthy and charitable in his formal behavior—will be due to the power of demons. This is an example of the blind leading the blind."

How to View the Sayings of the Ancestors

A QUESTIONER ASKED: "It is said that when looking at the sayings and teachings of the buddhas and ancestors, if you look
at them as one with fresh hatred looks upon an enemy, you will
then for the first time be able to understand them. What do you
think about this?"

Bassui: "The Way is a fundamental part of everybody. Its essence
is to penetrate enlightenment and to leave no trace of this attainment. If I were to explain this fundamental part, even the one word
awaken would add waves to a level surface. How much more so
with sayings and teachings? One who holds onto the residue, and
cannot grasp the real, cuts himself off from the source in the end.

"Buddha-nature, the self of all beings, is the simple truth as it is.
It transcends sects and rules. Even the buddhas of the three worlds
(past, present, and future) can't explain it. The commentaries on the
treasury of the teachings discussed during the lifetime of Shakyamuni Buddha can't catch hold of it either. Its full function has no
equal. The speed of a flint spark can't compare with it. Lightning
can't even penetrate it. Its activity has no fixed direction; thinking
it is rising in the east, it sinks in the west; thinking it is rising in the
south, it sinks in the north. It makes thunder roar in clear fine
weather and flames arise at the bottom of the sea.

"It is the master of seeing, hearing, and perceiving and the master that raises the hands and propels the legs. From the buddhas
and ancestors down to insects, of all things that possess essential

nature,[18] who would not receive its favor? What of you people? Do you know yourselves? When you doubt sufficiently, your enlightenment will be sufficient. When you have true aspiration, even if you don't want to doubt, your whole body will be filled with doubt; even if you don't seek expedient practices, your mind will not busy itself with miscellany. Though you don't want to eliminate them, you will be rid of the ten thousand things. Though you don't choose to discard them, reading sutras and commentaries and all kinds of activities will naturally be eliminated; profit and loss, good and bad, all will be obliterated. Like one who is stricken with a severe illness and is about to die, whose mind doesn't distinguish friends from enemies, when you travel, you will forget you are walking; when you are eating, you will be unaware of the taste; when you are sitting, you will forget you are sitting; forgetting your body, you will not lie down. If, in this way you become a part of this doubt, in a short time you will inevitably experience great enlightenment.

"If at this time you should meet a teacher of heretical ways, or seeing the strange words and queer phrases of the buddhas and ancestors your interpretive understanding is aroused and you arbitrarily cease doubting, it would be like facing the seashore and turning back. You would be like the one who resolves to starve himself to death but takes just one kernel of rice, and as a result is unable to put an end to the roots of his life. With this attitude one would not be qualified to penetrate enlightenment. That's why when you look at the sayings and teachings of the buddhas and ancestors, if you look as one with fresh hatred looks at his enemy you will for the first time be able to understand them. There are people, however, who interpret according to particular sayings and teachings, or understand based on consciousness and the activities of consciousness, their speech like a swiftly flowing stream. They are nothing but members of a family of demons, the kin of heretics. This increases their karma for birth in hell. We should pity them.

"When these people speak in this manner, it is as if they were scattering urine and excreta over the Pure Land. They have been floating and sinking in the sea of birth and death since time immemorial because they are not capable of ridding themselves of the casing that covers the treasure house of the true Dharma eye of the self as it is—a treasure house covered by many particles of dust of delusion from letters, words, and names. This is the great disease of ordinary people. This is why the buddhas and ancestors could not avoid persuading ordinary people in accord with their ability as a temporary measure. There are no fixed words with which they pull out the spikes and wedges of delusion. This is simply medicine in response to disease, waste paper to wipe off impurities. If you become attached to this, focusing your mind on a fine hair, it is like collecting waste paper, which will become impure, or medicine, which will become diseased. How will this ever be overcome? Though gold dust is valuable, in the eyes it causes cataracts."

If You Want Enlightenment…

BASSUI: "An ancient said:[19] 'To care for this matter as your own, be like a man who, passing through a village that has been infected with destructive rice worms, will not even wet his throat with a drop of water—then you will attain it.' Thus if you want enlightenment, abandon to its depths all ordinary attachment to deeds and behavior, principles and obligations, opinions and interpretations; be as before the birth of your mother and father, separate from all external phenomena, neither sinking into internal quiet nor settling in the void. Look directly! Now, as you are listening, tell me! What is it that listens?

"The priest Rinzai said: 'This physical body of yours composed of the four great elements can't hear the Dharma; your spleen, stomach, liver, and gallbladder can't hear the Dharma; the empty sky can't hear the Dharma.' Then what does hear it?' Just let go from the overhanging cliff and investigate thoroughly."

The Meaning of Looking at the Self with Hatred

A QUESTIONER SAID: "I hear that all the successive ancestors point directly to people's minds, causing them to look into their inherent nature and attain Buddhahood. I also hear that looking at one's self is as intense as hatred for an enemy. What is the meaning of this?"

Bassui replied: "In the self there are true and false. The discriminating mind is the false; Buddha-nature is true. When you awaken to your true nature, you cut off the roots of the wheel of transmigration, manifest your many inherent virtues, and make contact with others, bringing benefit to their lives. This is seeing into your inherent nature and attaining Buddhahood. The root of life and death is the discriminating mind. Beginning practitioners mistakenly take things like the [the ability to] emit light and perform miracles, which are really the roots of ignorance (being activities of the mind), for the clear expression of Buddha-nature. An ancient said:[20] 'Students of the Way don't realize the truth because they dwell on the discriminating mind of the past. The seed of birth and death through endless aeons is what fools call the true original self.'

"This discriminating mind is the boss of notorious robbers, the origin of the ten evil deeds, and the pit of knowledge based on attachment to form. If it is not destroyed, though you were to speak wonderful words of the miraculous, they would all be no more than strange spirits of wild foxes. In the end you wouldn't be able to avoid floating in the world of transmigration. That's why its destruction is connected with the one great matter. The reason for transmigration through the six realms of existence, from the beginningless beginning to the present, tossing and turning in great pain, is that you can't turn off this discriminating mind. The tree of swords and the mountain of blades are born of it; the boiling kiln and burning coal come from it also. The demons and devils too come from nowhere else. The beast with hair and horns is no other than a product of this discriminating mind. Though there are new heads and different faces, some dying here and being reborn there, though there may be retribution from various results of causes, some becoming beautiful and some becoming ugly, all are a result of nothing other than this discriminating mind. Though it is said never to have form, it is like fire that kindles flame in firewood when the proper contact is made. If this contact no longer exists, quiet sets in. When it moves, it is like clouds and mist appearing; when it is under control, it is like the clear blue sky. Though pure and impure are said to be different, they are of one root. Younger students mistakenly try to eliminate the impure when it arises, and they love the pure. They are like the man who, forbidden to drink liquor, feared impure liquor and loved pure liquor. One who is attached to the pure world, which is miraculous and illuminating, empty and calm, clear and bright, thinks he has awakened to his Buddha-nature, that he understands with his whole body, and there is not even a hair's worth of doubt to his understanding. It is like a man crazily drunk who gets excited over something, feels elated, and is sure it is his true mind [he sees and not just the effects of] liquor in his body; he wonders how he could ever be mistaken. When you are this drunk, whether you do good deeds or evil ones, all your behavior is that of a drunken mind, not a true one.

"As long as students of the Way haven't eradicated their discriminating minds, all their activities and words are the deeds of karmic consciousness; they are not in accord with the Way. Whether they are bright or dull, knowledgeable or ignorant, thoughtful or thoughtless, desirous or desireless; whether they use expedient means or study the teachings directly; whether they are venerated or held in contempt; whether they perform miracles and have feelings of love and pity—nonetheless, these are still activities of the discriminating mind.

"When it is cold, all heaven and earth are cold. When it is hot, all heaven and earth are hot. When there is justice, everything is just. When there is evil, everything is evil. When you stop the movement of the discriminating mind and realize the way of no-mind, whether you practice rightly or wrongly, speak or remain silent, are active or quiet, the self is never there; all is the turning of the right Dharma wheel. From the beginning there has never been evil and good with regard to the Dharma. Evil and good simply exist when you are trying to destroy the discriminating mind and you haven't done so. If you clearly eliminate the drunken mind, drunken rages will instantly stop and mind and body will be calm and quiet. If you want to recover completely from your illness, then stay free when sitting, lying down, and when doing walking meditation, and don't rely on another's power. Just stop your wandering, look penetratingly into your inherent nature, and, concentrating your spiritual energy, sit in zazen and break through to the self; then you will, for the first time, attain liberation. If you simply try to stop the movement of consciousness and consider this enlightenment, it will be like searching for a fish, considering it a jewel, or searching after a robber and treating him as your child. This will put an iron wall between you and enlightenment. It will be a hateful traitor damaging the Dharma treasure. That's why it is said that you must look at the self like one with fresh hatred viewing an enemy; only then will you succeed."

On Expedient Means

A QUESTIONER SAID: "Today I realize, for the first time, that all these years I have been searching after a robber and treating him as my child. Though I may see my mistake, if I do not actually destroy this discriminating mind myself, the moment of liberation will never arrive. With what expedient means will I rid myself of it?"

Bassui replied: "There is no particular expedient means. If you just separate from all forms in your mind and don't fall into the pit of formlessness, liberation will manifest in your body as it is right now. The high priest Mumon Ekai said:[21] 'To obey the regulations and keep the rules is to tie yourself without a rope. Arbitrary selfishness is heresy and devilry. Becoming settled and quiet while the mind exists is the heretical Zen of silent illumination. Doing as you will, neglecting relationships, you fall into the deep pit of liberation. To be clever and clearheaded is to be tied in chains, to be bound in shackles. To think of good and bad is to dwell in the temples of heaven and hell. Fixed views of the Buddha and Dharma enclose you in the two iron mountains.[22] One who has an instant awakening from an arising thought is sporting with spirits. Meditation in complete stillness is an activity of the devil. When you advance, you are deluded by Buddhist principles; when you retreat, you act contrary to Buddhist teachings. When you can neither advance nor retreat, you are a breathing corpse. Now, how on earth can you practice this after all?...[23]

"If you practice and realize this[24] now in this way, you will comprehend the great matter of life and death. If, however, you become

obstructed by the theory, and do not penetrate the gate of the ancestors, you will sink in the sea of delusion through eternity. This is why
the ancients, arousing their fearless aspiration, spent twenty, thirty,
or forty years—even their whole lives—refraining from lying down,
forgetting to sleep or eat, practicing single-mindedly, applying
spiritual energy in response to the occasion, looking penetratingly
into their own nature, and hence realizing the light of their own
spiritual essence. All karmic hindrances are founded in this discriminating mind, and this so-called discriminating mind is founded in
Buddha-nature.

"Master Rinzai said: 'I do not hold onto the worldly or the sacred
without, nor do I dwell on the substance within; I see penetratingly
and harbor no mistaken doubt.' Just look sharply during the four
dignified activities (walking, standing, sitting, and lying down) in
response to relationships and conditions. Hitting upon each opportunity, kill the mind that functions in that moment as you would an
enemy met on a narrow road. Be like one who not only tries to
smother a fire, but immediately pours water on the warm ash. If
even a fine hair were left unslain, you would be cast away in the
world of life and death. Turning inward, turning outward, destroying everything completely, you will for the first time begin to achieve
the proper results.

"Realize that all form is apparition, and stop calculating; realize
that all views are delusion, and kill the Buddha when he appears in
your mind and the ancestors when they appear in your mind and
ordinary people when they appear in your mind; destroy the world
when it appears and the void when it appears. At this time, though
you may understand all the worlds in the ten directions to be simply the one diamond essence, you will still fall into the trap of attachment to Dharma. Those who go beyond the ranks of ordinary
people, to the contrary, fall into the trap of considering themselves

sages. Though you cut off thoughts of both ordinary people and sages, though you do not stop before the cold withered tree,[25] though you cross the bright moonlit river and pass through the land of darkness,[26] if you think you have realized the mysterious functioning of the extraordinary, you still may not have let go of attachment to your ability. Forgetting the true flavor of the buddhas and ancestors and not realizing the universal essence, you sojourn in the cold ashes of the long smothered fire,[27] having yet to become intimate with the teachings.

"Do you wish to penetrate directly and be free? When I am talking like this, many people are listening. Quickly! Look at the one who is listening to this talk. Who is he who is listening right now?

"If, for example, you were to conclude that it is the mind, nature, Buddha, or the Way; if you were to call it the principle, the matter, the nontransmitted teaching of the buddhas and ancestors, the wonderful miracle, the occult, the mysterious, form, or emptiness; if you were to understand it to be existence and nothingness, nonexistence, non-nothingness, the absence of nonexistence, or the absence of non-nothingness; if you were to conclude that it is aeons of emptiness before creation or consider it the understanding of kōans, no-mind or noninterference, you would still be mixed-up ordinary people who haven't left the path of reason.

"If, on the other hand, you were to make a fist and raise a finger, clap your hands and remain silent, launch into an explanation according to your understanding, or present the main point as you see it, you would be nothing more than a fellow trifling with spirits, a ghost clinging to the bushes and weeds. When nothing you try applies, what is it that does, after all, listen to the Dharma? If you can't answer, you get thirty blows; if you do answer, you still get thirty blows. How can you manage to avoid suffering these blows? Well?"

That Which Hears the Dharma

A MONK SAID: "The discriminating mind is indeed like a dreaded enemy. What about when I look into my Buddha-nature? How shall I consider it?"

Bassui replied: "It too is like a dreaded enemy, because it destroys your body and ends your life."

The questioner asked: "What do you mean?"

And Bassui replied: "The mud cow impetuously enters the water against the current. The wooden figure plays with raging flames in its bosom pocket."

Questioner: "Master, you said earlier that the true teaching of the buddhas and ancestors is nothing other than pointing directly to peoples' minds and showing them that seeing into their own nature is Buddhahood. Now you talk neither of mind nor of nature. You just say we should look at that which listens to the Dharma. What does this mean?"

Bassui: "This is the true key to seeing into your own nature directly."

Questioner: "Is this phrase 'that which hears the Dharma' an expedient means created by you, master, or is it from the sayings of the buddhas and ancestors?"

Bassui: "It is neither my expedient means nor is it from the sayings of the buddhas and ancestors. It is the innate perfection of all people, the exquisite gate of emancipation of the buddhas and ancestors."

Questioner: "It has been said that what has not appeared in any of the texts since ancient times is no subject for discussion by wise men. If it has never appeared in the sayings of the buddhas and ancestors, who would believe it unquestionably?"

Bassui: "There are no words for the Way. That's why it is independent of the sayings of the buddhas and ancestors. Though it is innate to all people, words are used to express it. So how could it be contrary to the writings of the buddhas and ancestors?"

Questioner: "If that is so, then which sutra concurs with this teaching?"

Bassui: "At the Śūramgama meeting,[28] where many sages practiced and entered the gate, there were twenty-five perfections in all. The one gate—the so-called one who hears the Dharma just mentioned—was the perfection achieved by the bodhisattva Kannon. The bodhisattva Mañjuśrī, asked by the World-Honored One to comment on this gate, praised it and called it the primary gate. At this point Mañjuśrī said to Ananda: 'Though you have heard all the secret teachings of buddhas as countless as atoms, you have yet to eliminate the flow of desires and thus have been mistakenly holding onto all you have heard. Rather than entertaining what you have heard from the many buddhas, why don't you listen to the listener?'"

Questioner: "The buddhas and ancestors all taught people in accord with the opportunity, as one gives medicine in response to an illness. Why do you, master, not choose in accord with the opportunity, but rather tell us simply to perceive the one who is listening to the Dharma?"

Bassui: "This focusing on the one who is listening to the Dharma is the *dhāraṇī*[29] gate of all buddhas and ordinary people. If you penetrate this gate, regardless of whether your ability is great or little, all will be liberated. Therefore, in the sutra it is said:[30] 'Members of the assembly, Ananda, turn your function of hearing back toward yourselves and listen to the nature of the listener. This nature will become the supreme Way of emptiness. This is how perfection becomes an actuality. This is the one nirvana gate of the buddhas as numerous as the sands of the Ganges. All past Tathāgatas have realized themselves through this gate. All the present bodhisattvas are now entering it and becoming perfectly clear. And the practitioner of the future too should, in this way, depend on this Dharma. Not only Kannon, but I, Mañjuśrī, also confirmed the Way through this gate.'

"Mañjuśrī also said: 'To realize the mind of nirvana, Kannon's practice is the best. The many other expedient practices are all from the divine power of the Buddha used in particular circumstances to rid disciples of their delusions. They are for long-standing practitioners and should not be preached indiscriminately to those of shallow and deep understanding alike.'

"Also, in a discourse from the high seat,[31] Mumon Ekai said: 'Rinzai said to the congregation of monks, "The four great elements that make up your body can neither preach nor listen to the Dharma. Your spleen, stomach, liver, and gallbladder can neither preach nor listen to the Dharma. The empty sky can neither preach nor listen to the Dharma." The great priest Rinzai spoke in this manner like the many parents who chew the rice for their infants. Though this may be the case, who is it that preaches the Dharma? Who is it that listens to the Dharma? Here, if you grasp this entirely, you will complete your practice.' How can you say that this matter is not covered in the writings of the buddhas and ancestors? It is just this 'one who hears the Dharma' that is paramount among the perfections of the many sages. Why do these ignorant people remain deluded and find themselves unable to believe this?"

Questioner: "If it is as you've just said, then it is not the teaching transmitted outside of the scriptures and not through words. How can you, a Zen priest, use this teaching of the 'one who hears the Dharma'?"

Bassui: "You people now listening to this talk, does the one who listens come from the teaching of the Buddha? Does he come from the teaching of the ancestors?"

The monk bowed low and left.

What about You?

A MONK SAID: "All teachers everywhere give medicine in accord with the illness. You, master, give this one medicine to everybody. Wouldn't this cause people to descend into a cave?"

Bassui replied: "There are an infinite variety of medicines that can be given in response to illnesses. The poisons that kill people do not discriminate between those of slight and considerable ability. If one actually consumes this poison and loses his life, who will have descended into a cave?"

Questioner: "When we listen to all kinds of sounds, we are supposed to look penetratingly into the one who is listening. What if there isn't even one sound?"

Bassui: "Who is it that doesn't hear?"

Questioner: "I have no doubt as to the one who is listening to the Dharma. "

Bassui: "What is your understanding?"

The monk was silent.

Bassui spoke reprovingly: "Don't spend your life sitting in a ghost cave."[32]

Questioner: "Neither the buddhas nor the ancestors can understand the 'one who listens to the Dharma.'"

Bassui: "Put the buddhas and ancestors aside for a moment. What about you?"

The monk responded: "I too do not understand."

Bassui: "What is the reason behind the buddhas' and ancestors' lack of understanding?"

The monk said nothing.

Another monk said: "This one who listens to the Dharma is clearly before your eyes."

Bassui: "Don't get caught by Rinzai's three noncomprehensions.[33] Speak! What is it that hears the Dharma right before your eyes?"

He, too, said nothing.

Which Means Is Better?

A monk said: "Some good teachers nowadays just tell us to look into our own nature. Others tell us to look into the *watō*.[34] Which one is better?"

Bassui replied: "Originally these meaningful expressions were all the same. Since one thousand or ten thousand phrases simply become the one phrase of one's own nature, one's own nature is the foundation of the *watō*. Reach the roots and there is no lamenting the branches. That's why if beginning practitioners were to first look directly into their own nature, they would be able to pass all kōans naturally. You should know, however, that even though you clearly understand your own mind, if you can't penetrate the *watō* of the ancients, you still haven't realized enlightenment. That's why an ancient said:[35] 'Before one reaches attainment, it is more important for him to contemplate the meaning than the phrases. After one reaches attainment, it is more important for him to study the phrases than the meaning.'"

A monk asked: "Then, since we are beginning students, is it wrong for us to look into the *watō*?"

Bassui: "Which *watō* are you looking into?"

The monk responded: "One's original face before the birth of his mother and father."

Bassui replied: "Isn't this original face the root of your own nature at present? Your mistake comes from your making them another's words."

Another monk asked: "I am a beginning student and have been given the *watō* 'This mind is Buddha.'[36] Is this the mistake of my good teacher?"

Bassui responded: "This mind is Buddha right now. It is not a matter of your receiving a kōan of an ancient master. It is direct pointing to your own mind right now. This is not the mistake of your master. That's why Hyakujō said:[37] 'All words and sayings gently turn, returning to the self.' If you truly perfect enlightenment, realizing in this manner, not only would the rare words and wonderful phrases of buddhas and ancestors become the self, but there would be nothing in all creation that, after all, is not the self."

The monk said: "Then, in other words, if I desire to clarify my own mind I have to look at all creation?"

And Bassui replied: "No, you don't. The desire to clarify your own mind is for the sake of understanding the great matter of life and death. When your aspiring heart is ripe for this, seeing forms as they are and clarifying the mind, you will realize the Way through your contact with things. But if from the beginning you want to clarify the self, looking at all creation, you will lose your criterion for measurement and without fail enter the path of heretics. If you desire to clarify your own mind, look penetratingly into the origin of the one who hears all sounds right now. Where the thinking path is exhausted and the roots of life cease, there the self becomes tranquil and the time of life's fulfillment arrives. An ancient said:[38] 'When you return to the origin, you obtain the essence; when you follow the external light, you lose sight of the teachings.' And the high priest Mumon Ekai said: 'To study Zen, you must pass through the gate of the ancestors. To attain this uncommon realization it is necessary to exhaust the way of thinking completely. If you do not pass through the gate of the ancestors and do not exhaust the way of thinking, whatever you do will be like a ghost clinging to weeds and bushes.'"[39]

Living Words and Dead Words

A questioner said: "An ancient said:[40] 'If your understanding is based on living words, you will never forget. If your understanding is based on dead words, you will not be able to save yourself.' What does this mean?"

Bassui replied: "In understanding based on dead words, function does not exist apart from the context. If your understanding is based on living words, it is because you have exhausted the path of thinking."

Questioner: "Are the words 'the one who hears the Dharma' dead words or live ones?"

Bassui: "Revered monk!"

Questioner: "Yes?"

Bassui: "Was that alive or dead?"

Questioner: "A buffalo passes by the window. His head, horns, and four legs all go by; why can't his tail go by?[41] Is this a dead phrase or a live one?"

Bassui: "For the present I will ask all of you what you see as the principle. Each one of you should state your own understanding."

One monk said: "Some beautiful fish pass through the net and remain in the water."

Another one said: "To experience liberation is quite easy, but to walk the path of the liberated is difficult."

And another said: "The buffalo is the Dharma body of the pure self. Since it is beyond past and present, both outside and inside, we can say that the tail can't go by."

Yet another said: "This is an enlightened student who still can't forget the traces from recognition of enlightenment." And one more said: "Though one clearly realizes the nature of the self, he still can't forget past habits."

The master lit into them in a loud voice: "Wrong! Wrong! Though this was originally a live phrase, when you interpret it with your ordinary mind, it becomes a dead phrase. This is no longer the gate of the ancestors but rather a parable of the Dharma gate. When you look at a live phrase with the interpretation of an ordinary mind in this manner, you banish this true teaching of our sect to another land. Though many have been writing their interpretations of this phrase for more than ten years, not one has come up with anything in agreement with this ignorant monk's understanding."

At this time the assembly said dumbfoundedly: "People like us can only respond in this manner. Please, master, say a turning word[42] in our stead."

The master, speaking in their stead, said: "If you meet a dead serpent on the road, don't kill it. Pile things in a bottomless basket and bring them back home."[43]

Then a questioner said: "'A thousand mountains are covered with snow. Why is there one lone peak that is not white?' Is this a dead phrase or a live one?"

Bassui asked: "How do all of you understand it?"

Again each one stated his understanding:

"I see it as the guest [i.e., discrimination] within the host [i.e., equality]."[44]

"I see the thousand snow-capped mountains as phenomenon and the lone peak as the one road advancing toward the absolute."

"I see them as the true mind and the deluded mind."

"I see the lone peak as the absolute and the thousand snowcapped mountains as the relative."

"I see it as simply having no particular meaning."

"I see it as a means of arousing doubt in the practitioner—an expedient means to make him implement some kind of practice."

Finally Bassui said: "All of these views too are deluded views of a rational consciousness. If they were correct, every farmer would already understand Zen. Don't you feel ashamed? When people who can't remove themselves from the dark human world contemplate the live phrases of the ancestors, these phrases become dead ones. It is difficult to avoid blame for this."

Bassui created this verse to illustrate his point:

> A thousand mountains, ten thousand peaks, snow piled high.
> A lone peak, why isn't it white?
> Guest–host, relative–absolute, fall into calculating.
> Go directly to this phrase:
> "An iron tree blooms with flowers." [45]

Bassui then said to the congregation: "The sixth ancestor said: 'Neither the wind nor the flag moves, the minds of the two monks move.'[46] Tendai Tokushō expressed his understanding of these words by saying: 'If neither the wind nor the flag moves, your mind moves arbitrarily. If you reject this immobility of flag and wind, you should clearly understand this place where they move. Or it is said: "Form is emptiness." Or: "This place where the wind and flag do not move, what is it?" Or: "If you try to clarify the mind through things, don't search after them." Or: "If you say one should understand that neither wind nor flag moves, you've already parted with the meaning of the ancestor." If none of these various interpretations is correct, how shall we fully comprehend it? If you truly understand this, what Dharma gate would not be open to you?'"[47]

"You should know that in the past as well as the present those who have not clarified the great Dharma have all aroused these kinds of discriminating feelings, staining the living words of the ancestors. Though it may be a dead phrase, if a 'living being' were to work with it, it would immediately become a live phrase. This is what is meant when it is said: 'If you understand how to treat it, even a dead serpent will come to life again.' Do you understand?

"Suigan[48] had an interview with the high priest Jimyō.[49] Jimyō asked: 'What is the true import of the Buddhadharma?' Suigan answered: 'When the clouds do not appear above the mountain peaks, the moon is reflected in the heart of the waves.'[50] Jimyō responded reproachfully: 'Are you going to express this view until your hair turns white and teeth turn yellow?' Whereupon Suigan's whole body broke out in a sweat and he was bewildered. Jimyō then said: 'You ask me.' Suigan asked: 'What is the true import of the Buddhadharma?' Jimyō answered: 'When the clouds do not appear above the mountain peaks, the moon is reflected in the heart of the waves.' Immediately upon hearing these words Suigan had a great enlightenment.

"According to Suigan's original viewpoint, the enlightened mind-moon clearly pervades, spreading throughout worlds as numerous as the sands of the Ganges, because the clouds of deluded thinking stop and thoughts are unborn. But since Suigan explained the 'true meaning of the Buddhadharma' with the deluded mind of one who plays with spirits, he was scolded by Jimyō. The great priest Jimyō's response was a living phrase of one who cut off the many streams of deluded thoughts. That's why it gives life to people.

"Now let me take some time to question all of you. What is it in this one phrase that divides it into a dead one and a live one? What is the principle behind the great priest Jimyō's 'When the clouds do not appear above the mountain peaks, the moon is reflected in the heart of the waves'? Look carefully into the meaning without sinking to the vision of the yet-to-be-enlightened Suigan. Though it is difficult to point out all the differences between dead phrases and live ones to beginning practitioners, in general, when through parables and proverbs the true essence of the mysterious Buddhadharma is reduced to definitions, it becomes a dead phrase. This is because the potential to understand is not independent of the context. Thus an ancient worthy said:[51] 'When there is a phrase in the phrase, it is a dead phrase. When there is no phrase in the phrase, it is a live phrase.' Another ancient said:[52] 'If the function of your *ki* (vital energy) is not independent of your degree of attainment, you sink in the sea of poison. If your words do not shock the masses, you sink into the river of the mundane.' Generally a live phrase does not become a dead one because of a mistake in the words of the phrase; rather it is because the one who studies it has not yet penetrated into his own nature.

"If you realize your error now, then abandon everything, return to your Self, and look attentively. Who, after all, is this one who comprehends the words of this phrase?"

MUD AND WATER MIXED TOGETHER

A QUESTIONER SAID: "There are the dead and the living with regard to phrases. Are there, however, the dead and the living with regard to the true nature of the one spirit?"

Bassui replied: "Mud and water mixed together."

The questioner asked: "What is the mind seal of the ancestors?"

And Bassui responded: "Eyebrows grow from a solid rock."

When It Is Cold, All Heaven and Earth Are Cold

Q UESTIONER: "Master, when you teach people, going into detail, you enumerate so precisely that even beginning practitioners arouse intellectual views as their practice develops. When you teach of advancement toward enlightenment, you are so progressive that even long-time practitioners do not know where to position themselves. Thus there are critics who say that your approach causes them to regress instead. How, master, do you escape blame for this?"

Bassui: "When it is cold, all heaven and earth are cold; when it is hot, all heaven and earth are hot. How are heaven and earth to blame?"

Questioner: "Is the master the same as heaven and earth?"

Bassui: "Do you see me or don't you?"

The monk hesitated.

Bassui: "Blind fool!"

Questioner: "What is the Way of the Zen sect?"

Bassui: "The eastern hall, the western hall."[53]

Questioner: "A monk asked Jōshū: 'Does a dog have Buddha-nature?' Jōshū answered: '*Mu.*' What does this mean?"

Bassui: "I will wait for Mount Fuji to smile, and then I will answer you."[54]

Questioner: "What is the quality of the master's realization?"

Bassui: "Yesterday's rain, today's wind."

Questioner: "A practitioner said: 'The original form cannot be protected.' What does this mean?"

Bassui: "A broken mirror does not reflect light."[55]

Evil Thoughts Are Born of Delusion

A QUESTIONER SAID: "An ancient said:[56] 'The one spirit is this skin pouch;[57] this skin pouch is the one spirit.' Is this correct?"

Bassui replied: "Yes it is."

Questioner: "If that is so, who will become a buddha after the body's dispersion into the four elements? Who will sink into the sea of transmigration? And what would be the rationale for keeping the precepts that prevent crime?"

Bassui: "If you continue holding this view in which you deny cause and effect, like an arrow you will fly straight to hell. Do you have dreams?"

Questioner: "When in a dead sleep, I usually dream."

Bassui: "What do you usually see in your dreams?"

Questioner: "It's not always fixed, but I usually see things that occur in my mind and through my body."

Bassui: "The rising and sinking after death are also like that. All thoughts that occur in the mind come by way of the four elements that comprise this physical body. Dreams in the night follow suit and appear in accord with good and bad thoughts of the day. Depending on the severity of the three karmic activities of the body, mouth, and mind, you rise or sink after death. That's why an ancient said: 'You receive a body according to your karma, and your body in turn produces karma.' Here you should realize the continuity of the body in this life with the body in the next one. If you truly understand this, you cannot doubt the statement, 'The one spirit is this skin pouch; this skin pouch is the one spirit.'"

Questioner: "I now realize, for the first time, that the body and mind are not separate. This being the case, the significance of 'seeing into your own nature is Buddhahood' is relegated to the leaves and branches. If you simply stop doing bad deeds concerning this physical body, practice various good deeds, keep the precepts, purify yourself, and eliminate evil thoughts, won't you then become a Buddha?"

Bassui: "All evil thoughts are born of deluded feelings. If you do not see penetratingly into your own nature, though you try to eliminate evil thoughts you will be like one who tries to stop dreaming without waking from his sleep. All deeds are rooted in deluded feelings. If you cut out the roots, how can the leaves and branches grow?"

Questioner: "Do you mean that one who sees penetratingly into his own nature and dismisses deluded feelings from his mind, though he conducts himself in a manner contrary to the precepts, would still not be guilty of sin?"

Bassui: "If he were a man who penetrated his own nature, how could he think of committing a sin in which he breaks precepts?"

Heretical Views of Nonexistence, Constancy, and Naturalism

A QUESTIONER ASKED: "If one were truly able to attain an empty mind, would he return directly to the void, never to be born again?"

Bassui responded: "That is the view of nonexistence[58] held by heretics and those of the two vehicles.[59] Of what value could this be to one who has obtained the Way? Actually, holders of this view are inferior to dogs and wild foxes."

The questioner continued: "Then for one who has attained the Way and realized the unborn and undying, is there no limit to the length of time he will be saving others?"

Bassui replied: "That is the view of constancy held by heretics.[60] This is not the meaning of the Buddhist explanation of unborn and undying. If you can detach yourself from both views of nonexistence and constancy, you will not be stained by life and death, you will come and go as you please, you will be the transformation body as you are,[61] you will save ordinary people in response to the situation, and, abiding by the power of prayer, you will be free."

Questioner: "But if the 'one spirit is this skin pouch; this skin pouch is the one spirit' applies to buddhas, ancestors, and ordinary people alike, and if there is no mind-nature outside of this, then rising, standing, moving, and being quiet, seeing, hearing, recollecting, and knowing are simply the natural activities of heaven. What is the need of seeing into one's own nature?"

Bassui: "That is the heretical view of naturalism.[62] If you do not clarify your Buddha-nature, you will get caught by the illusory body, thinking it is real. Not even in your dreams would you then understand the principle of one's true nature being one with phenomena. The 'one spirit is this skin pouch; this skin pouch is the one spirit' would mean no more than ordinary people's attachment to existing phenomena."

Questioner: "Buddha-nature was before heaven and earth. It is the root of all buddhas and ordinary people. It fills limitless empty space. All things are proof of this One Dharma. Thus when the World-Honored One was born he took seven steps in the four directions, pointed to heaven and to earth, and said: 'Above and below heaven only I, alone, am revered.' I do not doubt this truth. Is it not 'seeing into one's own nature'?"

Bassui: "That is not true enlightenment either. It is simply a view of the area bordering on the shadows. Remember Ummon's words: 'If I had seen it,[63] I would have beaten him to death, fed his corpse to a dog, and made the world peaceful.'"

Questioner: "This view is not superficial. It's just that Ummon hated the egocentric aspect of the statement, 'I alone am revered.'"

Bassui: "You are a theorist. You have yet to understand the import of the Right Law. If actual enlightenment accompanied birth, why would the Buddha have entered the Himalayas, eaten only barley and the berries of the hemp plant, and sat in meditation for six years, forgetting his body and mind while reeds pierced his thighs, before finally having a great realization on the morning of the eighth day of the twelfth month?"

Questioner: "The World-Honored One's six years of sitting meditation was an expedient means for the purpose of leading ordinary people."

Bassui: "If you call this an expedient means, then to call something an expedient means is itself another expedient means. Where will it end?"

Questioner: "If all viewpoints are thus incorrect, what is correct?"

Bassui: "In the *Sutra of Perfect Enlightenment* it is written: 'Virtuous men, even those minds that realize the wisdom of the Tathāgata and verify the pure unstained nirvana are all aspects of the ego.'"

Questioner: "Then if you attain an empty mind straightaway, will you advance on the fundamental path toward enlightenment?"

Bassui: "Though students of the Way attain an empty mind and remain tranquil, when it comes to seeing with the true Dharma eye, their empty mind takes them even deeper into a hole."

Questioner: "What about passing directly through the ten thousand barriers and going beyond the empty mind?"

Bassui: "A cloud above Godaisan Mountain,[64] rice steaming, a dog in front of the old Buddha hall urinating in heaven."

THE TITLE

WHEN THE MASTER WAS LIVING in the province of Kō in Enzan, he was attended by a certain monk who brought him a manuscript and said: "Recently I have been recording a small portion of the instruction that, in response to their questions and doubts, you have given to monks, nuns, and laypeople. At this time I have compiled three volumes. Though I have forbidden it, the number of people who go away having copied these notes grows larger and larger. Thus they pass them around without permission, and others write them down. Because of this, a bird becomes a horse when the characters are written, changing the meaning of the whole as well.[65] In the end, a person who sees it acts in error and, contrary to his intentions, commits a sin. It is for this reason I would like to print official copies. I would also like to add the simplified *kana* script so it can be read easily by those not so literate. Please, master, think of a name for the title."

The master responded: "Printing this was not my idea. What name can I consider for the title of such a coarse mixture of mud and water? Nevertheless, if you want to use it to instill courage and caution in future generations, call a craftsman and entrust the printing to him."

Thus it is called *A Collection of Mud and Water from Salt Mountain*.

PART IV

QUESTION YOUR MIND

IF YOU WANT TO AVOID the suffering of life and death, you must know the way to Buddhahood this very moment. The way to Buddhahood is to realize your own mind. Your own mind is the original face before the birth of your parents; consequently before your own birth. It is the original nature of all beings that has remained unchanged up to the present.

This mind is originally pure. It was not born with this body and does not die with its extinction. What's more, it cannot be distinguished as male or female, or shaped as good or bad. It is beyond any comparison so we call it Buddha-nature. Moreover, like waves from the ocean, the many thoughts arise out of this original nature. They are like reflections from a mirror. That's why you must first see where thoughts come from if you want to understand your mind. So whether asleep or awake, standing or sitting, you must question deeply, "What is this mind?" The deep desire to realize this is called religious practice, training, aspiration, or the Way-seeking mind. Questioning your mind in this manner is also referred to as zazen.

Seeing your own mind even once surpasses reading incalculable sutras and dharanis every day for countless years. These formal practices serve merely to bring about good fortune. But when the good fortune is spent, you will again incur suffering of the three evil paths.[1] Since this practice [of seeing into your own mind] will ultimately lead to enlightenment, it is the seed of Buddhahood. Even one who commits any of the ten evil deeds or the five cardinal sins,[2] for example, upon realization through self-reflection can become a Buddha instantly.

But don't think then that you can commit sins while relying on the prospect of enlightenment. If you delude yourself and fall into hell, neither Buddha nor ancestors can save you. Take the example of a young boy sleeping next to his father. If the boy dreams that someone is beating him or that he has become sick and he calls out to his father and mother for help, since they can't enter his dream world they can't help him. Even if they wanted to give him medicine, they couldn't do it without waking him from his dream. If he were to awaken himself, he would escape the torment of the dream without the help of anyone. In a similar way when you realize that your own mind is Buddha, you immediately escape [the painful world of] birth and death. If the Buddha could have saved them, would even one sentient being have fallen into hell? You will never understand this if you don't wake up yourself.

When you ask yourself who the master is who this very moment sees with the eyes, hears with the ears, raises the hands, moves the feet, you realize that all these operations are the work of your mind. But you don't know why it works this way. You may say it doesn't exist, but it is clear that something is freely functioning. You may say it does exist, but then you can't see it. Now when this [inquiry] feels insurmountable and you are unable to understand anything, when you have exhausted all ideas and don't know where to turn, you are proceeding correctly. Don't let yourself fall back at this time. As you pursue this inquiry more deeply, your piercing doubt will penetrate to the depths, ripping through to the bottom, and you will no longer question the fact that your mind is Buddha. There will be no [world of] life and death to despise and no truth to seek. The world of the great void will be the one mind.

If you dream, for example, that you have lost your way and can't find the road home, though you may ask people and pray to the gods or to the Buddha, you still won't be able to find your way back. But if you wake from that dream, you will realize that you are in your own bed. Then you will see that in order to return from your dream travels, all you have to do is wake up—and there is no other way. This is called returning to your roots, going back to the source. It is also referred to as being born in the world of peace. It is obtained as a result of the power from a certain degree of religious practice.

One who enjoys practicing zazen and who takes part in religious practices, whether it be as a lay follower or clergy, is endowed with the ability to understand this. But one who doesn't practice will never understand. However, if you think that this degree of realization is true enlightenment, in which you no longer doubt your understanding of the true nature of reality, you will be making a great mistake. It will be like giving up hope of finding gold because you discover copper.

If you feel yourself giving up in this way, you must gather your courage and inquire deeply, seeing your body as a phantom, as a reflection of foam on water. See your mind as the empty sky, having no form. Ask who is the master that hears voices and recognizes echoes within this emptiness—never letting up even for a moment, questioning deeply and relentlessly. In the end, understanding through reason will completely disappear and you will forget your own body. Then your previous ideas will cease and the depth of your questioning mind will be sufficient. Your realization will be as complete as when the bottom falls out from a barrel and not a drop of water remains. It will be like a flower blooming on a dying tree. Then you will be a person who has attained freedom through the Buddhadharma; you will be a liberated person.

But even though you may have realized in this manner, you must have this kind of realization many times and throw it out, returning to the one who realizes. When you return to the source and guard it mightily, exhausting discriminating feelings, your own true nature will come to life. Like a jewel getting brighter with repeated polishing, [constantly return to the one who realizes and] the brilliance of your realization will increase, and in the end you will brighten the whole world in the ten directions. Never doubt this!

If your aspiration for the way is not deep enough and you don't attain realization in this lifetime, if you die while in the middle of your practice, you will easily attain realization in your next life as surely as one who today executes work that was planned yesterday.

When you practice zazen, neither despise nor delight in thoughts that arise. Simply look into their source and know that everything that appears in your mind or is seen through your eyes is illusion, devoid of reality. Don't fear it, don't revere it, don't love it, and don't hate it. When you keep your mind unmarked like the empty sky, at the time of your death you won't be harmed by demons. But don't hold any of this teaching in your mind when practicing, just continue to inquire into [the nature of] your mind. Also when you realize who the master is that hears all voices this moment, your mind is the source of all buddhas and ordinary people.

Because Kannon attained realization by hearing the [source of] voices, she was named, "The Bodhisattva Perceiver of Sounds." When standing or sitting, see what it is that hears voices—while doing this you will lose sight of the hearer. While continuing to pursue this, you will reach an impasse and lose your direction. At that time, while sounds can still be heard, look more deeply into what it is that hears. In this state continue to exert yourself to your limit and you will be like a clear, cloudless sky.

At this time there will be nothing you can call the self. You will see the one who hears. Your mind will be one with the vast empty sky. But, in fact, there will be nothing you can call the empty sky. You will think this is realization, but here too you should seriously question! Who is it now that hears sounds?

When you cease creating thoughts, skillfully proceeding so that even the understanding of an objectless empty sky vanishes, you shouldn't retreat in the face of this darkness, but rather ask yourself again what it is that hears sound. When you have exhausted all your energy, amply doubting, you will break through your doubts like a dying person being revived at the last moment. *This* is realization.

Now for the first time you will become one with the buddhas and ancestors. If you have gotten to this point, look at the following:

A monk asked Jōshū, "What is the meaning of the ancestor coming to the West?

Jōshū responded, "The oak tree in the garden."

If you hesitate for a moment, return to inquiring as to the one who hears sounds. If you don't clarify this in your present life, when will you? If you lose this human birth, you may not escape the eternal pain from the three evil paths. What is obstructing realization? Understand that obstruction will only result from your lack of aspiration for the Way. Practice with vitality!

To a Man from Kumasaka

YOU ASKED ME to teach you how to practice during your illness. Who is it that is ill? Who is it that is practicing? Do you know who you are? Your whole body is Buddha-nature. Your whole body is the great Way. The true foundation of this Way is pure and divorced from all features. What form of illness could it possess? It is the source of all buddhas, the mind of all beings, the original face. It is the master who sees, hears, awakens, and knows. If you realize this, you are a buddha. If you don't realize it, you are an ordinary being. That's why all the buddhas and ancestors pointed directly to the mind—so that people can see their own nature and realize Buddhahood. It's like one who is lost in shadows; all you can do is show him the true form.

In ancient times there was a man who thought he saw a snake in his glass of alcohol, but he drank it anyway. No sooner had he returned to his house than he began to feel unbearable pain. He tried various remedies but to no avail. When the host [at whose house he had drunk the alcohol] heard about it, he called the man back, placing him in the same seat he was in when he drank the alcohol. The host then gave him more alcohol telling him that it was medicine for his stomach problem. As the man was about to drink, he noticed a snake in the cup, just like the previous time. When the guest informed his host of this fact, the host pointed above the place where his guest sat. Above the spot was a bow hanging from the ceiling. Realizing that what he saw as a snake was really a reflection, he looked at his host, and the two of them laughed without saying a word. The pain disappeared, and the man was back to normal.

Seeing into one's nature and realizing Buddhahood is also like this. Yōka[3] said: "Realize the truth and there is neither person (subject) nor Dharma (object). At that moment the karma of the lowest hell will be extinguished."

The true body is the origin of all beings. If you don't believe that your mind is the perfect realization of the Tathāgata and you attach to existing phenomena, seeking the Buddha and Dharma elsewhere, though you practice various forms of asceticism in order to realize Buddhahood, since you will not have eliminated the workings of the ego you will suffer the pain of countless transmigrations in the three worlds.[4]

Just as if you'd thought that you'd drunk a snake with your alcohol and had become extremely ill, if you do nothing other than see the source [of the illusion] you will immediately be rid of the illness. Therefore all that is needed is that you see your own mind. Nobody can give you this Dharma.

It is said in the *[Perfect Enlightenment] Sutra:* "Know that the enemy is illusion and you won't need to rid yourself of anything." All phenomena are illusion; none are real. All buddhas and ordinary people are images reflected on the water. When you see these reflections as reality, it is because you are not seeing your true nature. A common mistake occurs when you control your thoughts, feel a vast quiet, and think that that is your original face. That too is a reflection of an image in the water. Simply go beyond rational thinking and you will reach a point where you will not know what to do. Inquire there. Who is it [who inquires]? You will know him intimately when you have broken your walking stick and crushed ice in a fire. Now, how do you achieve this intimacy? Today is the eighth day and tomorrow is the thirteenth![5]

To the Abbess of Jinryōji Temple

One who aspires to Buddhahood must know the master of she who aspires. If you want to know the master, you must inquire into the foundation of your present thought; who thinks about what is good and what is bad, who sees form and who hears voices. If you question [these things] deeply, you will definitely understand. If you understand, you will be a Buddha this instant. Realization of Buddha *is* the one mind of all beings. Its essence is pure and cannot be stained by external objects. Though it may exist in a woman's body it does not have female characteristics. Though it may exist in a man's body it does not have male characteristics. Though it may exist in a wretched body it is not lowly. Though it may exist in a noble body it is not regal. Like a vast emptiness it has no color. Even if heaven and earth were to be destroyed, this vast emptiness would remain colorless and formless. It reaches every corner of the earth. The one mind too is like this.

This one mind is not born with the physical body, nor does it die with the demise of the body. Though it can't be seen, it operates through the whole body, seeing with the eyes, hearing with the ears, smelling with the nose, speaking with the mouth and propelling the hands and legs. There isn't any place where it doesn't function. Seeking the Buddha and Dharma outside of this mind is called the delusion of ordinary people. A buddha is one who understands that this very body is Buddha. That's why nobody will attain Buddhahood who doesn't realize her own mind.

Every being in the six realms[6] without exception possesses this mind just as the open sky reaches everywhere. Nothing is apart from it. This is affirmed by the statement, "In Buddha there is no discrimination."

In order to teach ordinary people about the one mind, knowing their basic ignorance and their attachment to existing phenomena, and therefore their lack of understanding of the nonexisting Dharma of the unstained true Buddha, when the various buddhas talked they sometimes called this Dharma the mani-pearl,[7] sometimes The Great Way, sometimes Amida Buddha, sometimes The All Pervading Buddha of Great Wisdom, sometimes The Bodhisattva Jizo,[8] sometimes The Bodhisattva Kannon, sometimes The Bodhisattva Fugen,[9] and sometimes your original face before the birth of your parents. For the sake of ordinary people transmigrating in the six realms, Jizo, master of the six senses, enters these worlds to teach the Way. All the epithets of the buddhas and bodhisattvas are the different names for this one mind. When you believe that your mind is Buddha, you will believe all the various buddhas. Thus it is stated in the *Kegon Sutra [Flower Garland Sutra]*, "The three worlds are simply the one mind. There is no Dharma outside of this mind. There are no distinctions among mind, Buddha, and ordinary people.

All sutras are words pointing to this mind for the sake of ordinary people. So one who sees the one mind for herself is like one who has read all the sutras in one breath. Thus it is written in the *Sutra of Perfect Enlightenment*, "Sutras are like fingers pointing to the moon," referring to all sutras. The finger pointing to the moon is directing ordinary people to their one mind. The one mind lights up the world. So when it is said that if you read a sutra you will receive great merit, this merit is the knowledge of the teaching [of this one mind].

It is also said that offering religious services to the Buddha leads to realization. This means realizing your mind. The acts of reciting the Buddha's name and reading sutras are rafts taking one to the shore of awakening. After riding in a raft across the river to the shore, one should discard the raft and hurry on. Thus it is said that seeing the one mind for a moment far surpasses the reading of sutras for ten thousand days. What's more, seeing your own mind greatly surpasses listening to this reasoning for ten thousand years. However, since one must proceed from shallow to deep, helpless fools and sinners who earnestly read sutras and recite names of buddhas can for the first time ride this raft. This is a fortunate development for them. But if they hang around the raft not thinking to proceed to the shore of enlightenment, they will be making a grave mistake.

Shakyamuni Buddha performed various ascetic practices without ultimately reaching an awakening; then he threw these practices out and did zazen for six years and realized his own mind. Reaching unsurpassed perfect awakening, he taught ordinary people the mind-Dharma. His discourses are called sutras and are words about the realization of one's mind. This one mind abides in the hearts of everyone and is the master of the six senses. Realization of this fact eradicates, in a flash, all karmic retribution like [a great block of] ice put into boiling water. After such realization you will know that your mind is Buddha. Though you may say that your mind is originally pure and there is no distinction between buddhas and ordinary people, deluded thinking creates distinctions much the same as clouds cover the light of the sun and the moon. But the power of practice can eradicate delusions as the wind sweeps away clouds. Buddha-nature manifests when deluded thinking ceases as if emerging from behind disappearing clouds. It is simply the appearance of primordial light. It did not come from somewhere else.

So if you want to avoid suffering through cycles of birth and death, just rid yourself of thoughts and feelings. If you want to rid yourself of thoughts and feelings, realize your own mind. If you want to realize your own mind, do zazen. Zazen is the essence of religious practice. To practice you must inquire deeply into the meaning of kōans. The source of kōans is your own mind. The deep desire to realize this mind is called aspiring mind or mind of the Way. One who deeply dreads falling into hell is called a man of wisdom. Those who do not aspire to the Buddha Way are like that because they know nothing of the sorrows of hell.

In ancient times there was a bodhisattva who, when she was in the form of a woman, attained realization through contemplation of all voices. The World-Honored One named her the Bodhisattva Who Hears All the Voices in the World (Kannon). If people today want to know the essence of "this mind is Buddha" when they hear a sound, they should see who it is that hears. Surely they will not be different from Kannon.

The mind is neither existent nor nonexistent; though it transcends form it isn't formless. Don't try to stop thoughts from occurring, but don't encourage thinking when thoughts do occur. Let them occur when they occur and cease when they cease. Don't get caught up in thought. Just inquire earnestly: "What is this mind?" Why do I say inquire earnestly? For the sake of enlightenment.

If you want to know the unknowable, your mind will be challenged until you reach a precipice. When you don't know what to do next, it is the optimal time to do zazen. When you are sitting, question in this way. Whether you are sitting or standing, whether you are awake or asleep, never forget that you haven't realized your own self, and inquire until you penetrate to the foundation. This is called religious practice. When you practice earnestly, penetrating this inquiring mind to its foundation, you will suddenly break through your doubts, and the truth that this mind is Buddha will manifest just as a mirror in a box can only reveal its reflections after the box is opened. The mirror will light up the world in the ten directions, leaving no place in the dark. Then for the first time transmigration through the sixth realms will cease and the harmful results of bad karma will be extinguished. It is difficult to describe in words the joy that this moment will bring to the heart. This is like a man dreaming that he is in prison and being tortured unbearably: at that moment he wakes up and all his suffering is gone. We can say that he was then free of the world of transmigration.

To realize this matter does not depend on the individual's ability; it depends on the person's aspiration. Buddhas and ordinary people are like liquid water and ice. In its ice state, water is like a rock tile having no freedom of movement. If it melts it returns to its original liquid state and is no longer rigid. Delusion is like ice. Enlightenment is its original exquisite form. There is no part of the ice that is not [in essence] water. You should understand that there is not an iota of distinction between ordinary people and buddhas. The only distinction is in deluded thought. When the deluded thought melts, the ordinary person is a buddha as she is. Never let feelings of indolence arise. If you believe, for example, that your aspiration is not strong enough to attain enlightenment in this life, but you continue to practice, encouraging yourself never to slacken, if you continue to practice up to the time of your death, you will surely attain enlightenment in your next life, just as things you begin today are easily completed tomorrow. So don't become negligent. What could you do to aid yourself if you were on your deathbed this moment? What could you do to avoid the karmic retribution of hell?

Fortunately there is a great Way that can free you. All the words I've used up to now are the branches and leaves. Now take this one phrase to your heart; find out why this mind is Buddha! If you want to know the essence of all the buddhas at a glance, simply realize your own mind. Is it true or false? Open your eyes and look right now. Why is this mind Buddha? If you realize this mind, the lotus blossom will open in the fire and won't wither in ten thousand world cycles. Everyone was originally in this lotus flower; why don't they know it?

To Gessō Seikō, Lord of Aki, from Nakamura

I RECEIVED YOUR LETTER asking how you should practice in order to understand the phrase "You must give life to the mind that has no dwelling place."

There is no particular approach to studying the Way. Just look directly into your nature and don't get involved in diversions, and the flower of your mind will bloom. Thus the sutra says, "Give life to the mind that has no dwelling place." The tens of thousands of phrases uttered by the buddhas and ancestors are just this one phrase. This mind is one's true nature distinct from all forms. Nature is the Way, the Way is Buddha, and Buddha is mind. This mind is not inside, it is not outside, and it is not in the middle. It is neither existence nor is it nothingness. It is neither nonexistence nor non-nothingness. It isn't mind, Buddha, or object. That's why it is called the mind that has no dwelling place.

This mind sees forms with the eyes and hears voices with the ears. You should simply study the master [of these processes]. An ancient master [Lin-chi I-hsüan] said, "The physical body made up of the four elements cannot discern the sermon you are listening to. The spleen, stomach, liver, and gallbladder cannot discern the sermon you are listening to. Empty space cannot discern the sermon you are listening to. What is it that can discern this sermon?" [Questioning] in this way, look directly!

If, when you look, your mind clings to any form or you become attached to a particular meaning and you spend your time conceptualizing, you will be as far from the Way as heaven is from earth. What do you do then to cut off the bonds of life and death? Advance and you'll get lost in reason; retreat and you'll violate the teaching. Neither advancing nor retreating, be like a functioning corpse ceasing [thinking] immediately and practicing without restraint. Surely then you will attain enlightenment and give life to the mind that has no dwelling place. Then you will clarify incomparably uncommon teachings including all the kōans and Dharmas.

Layman [P'ang Yun] Hō asked Ma-tsu Tao-i: "What kind of person has no friend among Dharmas?" Ma-tsu Tao-i replied: "I will respond to you when you have swallowed all the water in the West River in one gulp." Hearing this, Layman Hō was enlightened. Look! What does this mean? Does this refer to the statement, "You must give life to the mind that has no dwelling place" or does it refer to the one who is listening to the Dharma? If you still don't understand, ask yourself who is listening to the voice right now? Focus your energy and look this instant! Life and death are essential matters, impermanence moves swiftly on. Don't waste your time. It waits for no one.

Your mind is fundamentally Buddha. Realize it and you are Buddha. Lose sight of it and you are an ordinary person. Whether asleep or awake, whether standing or sitting, simply inquire, "What is my mind?" and look at the source where thoughts arise. Wondering what it is that understands things in this way, that propels this body, that performs work, that advances and retreats, ask yourself: "What is it, after all?" Aspire only to realize this yourself, constantly inquiring, never negligent, and even if you don't realize it in this lifetime you will surely do so in the next. Never doubt this!

When you decide to practice zazen, don't consider what is good or bad. When thoughts occur, don't try to stop them. Simply question immediately what this mind of yours is. Though you question deeply in this manner, no method will give you the knowledge. Remaining in a state of not knowing, the way through thinking will cease, you will lose all sense of a "me" in your body and you will realize that there is no thing you can call the mind. Asking what it is [that realizes], return to yourself and look. The mind that wants to know will disappear, as will all teaching, and you will be like the empty sky. When mind realizes that it is like the empty sky and penetrates to the depths, you will awaken to the realization that there is no buddha outside of this mind and there is no mind outside of the Buddha.

Now you will know for the first time that when you listen without your ears, you can truly hear, and when you see without your eyes, you can see all the buddhas from the past, present, and future. But these words taken as they are will not enlighten you. You have to actually realize this for yourself. Look, look! What is your mind? Be careful! Though it is said that fundamentally the original nature of people is naturally the Buddha, if you don't believe it and instead you seek the Buddha and the Way elsewhere, you will not attain enlightenment and will be pulled around by good and bad karma, not being able to escape transmigrating through endless cycles of birth and death.

The source of much karma is discriminating feelings. Put an end to discriminating feelings and you'll be free. If by realizing your own nature you extinguish these discriminating feelings, it will be like blowing on a fire buried in ash—the fire emerging and the ash eradicated.

When doing zazen don't be upset as thoughts occur, but don't savor them either. Just trace them back to their origin, looking at the source without letting it disturb you. If you do this and you eradicate discriminating feelings derived from the source of all thoughts, it will be like the destruction of ash in flames through fanning the fire. Though delusions are erased and nothing remains in your heart, though there is no separation between inner and outer, and though you are like a clear and empty sky, pure in all directions, this is not enlightenment. If you take this to be Buddha-nature, it would be like seeing shadows and thinking they are real. Now you will have to work more diligently at gathering your energy to look at this mind that hears sounds.

Your physical body composed of the four elements is like an illusion; it is not reality. The mind, however, is not apart from the physical body. The empty sky does not see forms nor does it hear voices. So what is it in you that hears voices and knows the different sounds? Ask yourself. Raise a great doubt until all discrimination between right and wrong is eliminated and views of existence and nothingness disappear like a light turned off on a dark night. Though you still may not know who you are, you know there is a self that hears all sounds.

Up to this point, though you tried to know what hears these sounds, it has eluded you. As you press the mind in every way, suddenly you will have a great awakening and be like a dead man revived, clapping your hands and laughing out loud. Then for the first time you will know that your mind is Buddha.

If I were asked what form "this mind is Buddha" takes, I would respond: The fish plays on top of a tree and the bird flies under water. What does this mean? If you don't understand, investigate yourself thoroughly. Who is the master that sees and hears? Don't waste your time. It waits for no one.

To a Dying Man

THE WONDROUS MIND-NATURE is not born and doesn't die. It neither exists nor is it nonexistent. It is neither formless nor does it have form. It feels neither pain nor pleasure. Though you want to know what it is that suffers now, in this way, it is something that can't be known.

If you just question what is this mind-body that suffers, thinking of nothing else, wishing for nothing else, and asking for nothing else, like a cloud disappearing from the sky, your mind will empty and you will cease transgressing the world of life and death and be immediately liberated.

To Layman Ippō Honma Shōgen

Yᴏᴜ ᴍᴇᴇᴛ ʜɪᴍ ꜰᴀᴄᴇ-ᴛᴏ-ꜰᴀᴄᴇ. Who is he? If you can answer, you're mistaken, and if you can't answer, you're still mistaken. What will you do after all?

"A calf is born on top of a flagpole." If you come to a realization at this point, you no longer need to exert excess energy. If you don't understand, return to your own mind and penetrate your Buddha-nature. Buddha-nature is the same in everyone; each person is perfect. Buddhas and ordinary people are equal; there are no distinctions between them. However, people in this world mistakenly tie themselves with their own ropes, saying, "We don't have the ability to understand our own nature. We can only read sutras, pray, and place our hopes in various buddhas, eventually entering the Buddha Way." And the listeners go along with this. As the saying goes, this is the blind leading the blind. This is not having faith in the Buddha and the sutras; it is slandering both. Why? Because silent reading of sutras means nothing more than looking at them. The Buddha is really another name for the mind-nature. It says in the *Kegon Sutra [Flower Garland Sutra):* "There should be no distinction among mind, Buddha, and ordinary people." This means that to say that you don't believe in your own mind but that you believe in the Buddha is the same as believing in an alias and not believing in the true body of the Buddha. This does not concur with the practice. Silent sutra-reading is equivalent to a starving person trying to relieve his hunger by looking at a menu rather than eating the rice gruel offered to him. All sutras are menus pointing to this true mind-nature.

It is said in the *Sutra of Complete Enlightenment:* "Sutras are like fingers pointing to the moon." How could the Buddha have ever intended for people to see the finger and not the moon? The [meaning of] the sutras is in every person. One look into your own nature without opening a sutra and even though you've never read a word you will understand the sutras in an instant. There are no exceptions. Isn't that the true sutra-reading?

Don't you see, the green bamboo is this very mind of the Way seeker? All those thickly grown yellow flowers are nothing other than *Prajna* [Wisdom]. Bowing is throwing down the ego-banner; the realization of your Buddha-nature. However, seeking Buddha-hood is not a result of how much you've learned. You have to realize who you are. There are those who believe this teaching and practice austerities, but not having attained enlightenment, at some point stagnate in the Way. There are others who stop the discriminating mind for a while and think their "no-thought" state is enlightenment. Still others think it enough to study one kōan constantly. There are others who never violate the precepts, seclude themselves exclusively in the mountains and call it the Way. And others say there is no particular Way of enlightenment: When tea is served, drink tea; when rice is served, eat rice. When they are asked about the Buddhadharma they give a shout or shake their sleeves and leave. They think that the Way means to have disregard for everything and to call those seeking out a good teacher dunces. If these people are students of the Way, then a three-year-old child could understand Zen.

There are some who say that when the light [from ideas] ceases and you no longer produce thoughts, becoming like a withered tree or a stone, this is the way of no-mind. Others say that when you empty your mind until there is no distinction between inner and outer and then, like the sun on a clear day, your mind shines, this light is a turning point. It is true that this is a result of your Dharma-nature appearing, but it is not enlightenment. The ancients call this the [confining] deep pit of liberation.

People with these views say that they have no doubts about the Way. They have lofty thoughts empty of real substance and love to debate Dharma, taking joy in winning arguments and losing their tempers when they are defeated. Resentful inside, they disregard the law of karma, speak loudly and chatter and enjoy amusing themselves while interfering with the religious practice of others. They see serious practitioners as dull, berating them with statements like "this is not the Zen sect." They are like crazy men laughing at the sane. Their self-aggrandizement grows daily and they fall into hell as quickly as a speeding arrow.

The First Ancestor said: "Those who say all is empty, knowing nothing of the law of cause and effect, fall into hell." Though their words may seem to make sense, these people can't do anything about their discriminating feelings. Often after a glimpse of their true nature, novice monks call it enlightenment. An ancient [Master Lin-Chi I-hsüan] said: "The body of Dharma-nature and the ground of Dharma-nature I clearly know to be reflections. Recognize the one who plays with these reflections; he is the primal source of all the buddhas."

Someone said to me: "Many concepts arise as a result of religious practice, and concepts are all sicknesses of the mind. If that is true, we cannot easily attain enlightenment. Even though we don't realize our own minds and don't understand the Buddhist sutras, yet we refrain from committing sins, will we still be punished? If while not attaining Buddhahood we don't fall into the three evil paths, is it still necessary to seek enlightenment?"

I responded: "The source of all sins is deluded feelings. You should never expect to erase these sins if you don't attain realization. The six roots [eyes, ears, nose, tongue, body, and mind] are a part of ordinary people. Each has one of the six rebels [form, sound, smell, taste, touch, and way] associated with it. Each rebel has three poisons—greed, anger, and foolishness. There are no living creatures that are not possessed of these three poisons. The three poisons are the causes and the three lower realms are the effects. Cause and effect are inevitably connected. Anyone who says he hasn't committed a sin doesn't understand this law. Even if you say that your present situation is not a result of them, the three poisons are originally a part of you. How much more those who add transgressions [in this life]?

Someone else asked me: "If all existing form is possessed of the three poisons, who among buddhas, ancestors, saints, and wise men can escape them?"

I responded: "Just wake up to your own nature, and the three poisons will be transformed into obeying the precepts, meditation, and wisdom. The buddhas, ancestors, saints, and wise men have all seen into their own nature. How could they commit any sins?"

Yet another person asked me: "A person who sees into his own nature transforms the three poisons into obeying precepts, meditation, and wisdom. How can one who suffers from the mind-sickness of deluded viewpoint be cured?"

I responded: "Seeing into your own nature is the one medicine for all diseases [of the mind]. There is no need for any other treatment. As I said before, that which knows the one who plays with reflections is the origin of all buddhas. One's Buddha-nature is like the jewel-sword of the Vajra King, causing instant death to whomever it touches. It's like a blazing fire taking the lives of all who come near.

If you see into your own nature even once, you will immediately sunder the ties of countless years of deluded karmic consciousness and lingering habits as ice placed over a burning fire will instantly disappear. At this time you will not even have a view of the Buddha or the Dharma much less any mind-sickness. The reason all delusions resulting from karmic hindrances and various discriminating thoughts and ideas are not erased is that you aren't aware of your true inherent nature. Hoping to avoid countless transmigrations while not having realized your inherent nature is like trying to stop water from boiling without removing the burning firewood [below it]. It makes no sense.

Fortunately you believe in the teaching outside of the scriptures and beyond words. What is the use then of trying to understand the verses [of the sutras]? Throw out all those interpretations of the teachings quickly and look directly within. Who is this master who sees and hears right now? If, as has hitherto been said, you call it mind, nature, Buddha, original face, existence, nothingness, emptiness, form, known, unknown, truth or ignorance, whether you use words or remain silent, whether you consider it enlightenment or delusion, you have missed the mark.

If you still doubt [the reality of this master] you will bind yourself without a rope. Though you try to understand it through the illusory process of labeling or verbally expressing it, you won't succeed. At the point when you try to express it but can't, return to questioning with your whole body and look penetratingly. Though you won't be able to find anything you can call your mind or your nature, still, when there is a sound you'll immediately hear it, and when someone calls out your name you'll immediately respond. It is right there: Who is it? When your thinking stops, your energy has been exhausted, and you don't know where to turn, continue forging ahead, and you will be like one who has let go of his grip and leaped into a deep pit of fire. If you proceed and are able to enter this fire of your indestructible original essence, your body, mind, and feelings, your discriminating thoughts along with your very life energy will be destroyed and your inherent nature will manifest; you will be like one who has died and is reborn, and then all ailments will be wiped away and you will attain peace and joy. You will be completely free. At that point you will realize that walking on water is like walking on earth and walking on earth is like walking on water. You could talk all day and wouldn't know you'd said a word. You could walk all day and wouldn't know you'd taken a step. You could eat all day and wouldn't know you'd taken a bite. In the southern mountains rain clouds would form and in the northern mountains it would rain. In China the [Dharma lecture] drum would sound and in Korea the high priest would take the high seat.[10] You would practice zazen in your small hut and would meet all the buddhas in the universe. Without looking at a single word you would understand the seven thousand volumes of sutras, receive all the merit and the good results of the many practices—all within that little body of yours. If you mistake this for supernatural powers, the day will come when you will have to lick molten iron in front of Yama.[11] If this isn't supernatural than what teaching does it express? Look at this carefully, right now!

To a Zen Student

Buddhas and ancestors cannot attain this unsurpassable wondrous Way, and ordinary people cannot lose it. Grasses and trees, tiles and pebbles are all your intimate friends. When you understand this completely, there is no need for cultivation. If you haven't yet understood this, you should step back and study your self. Well, what is it that you call your self? Look within, who is indeed speaking, complying, and practicing right now in this manner. Who is it? Whether you call it mind, nature, Buddha, Dharma, truth, falsehood, the path, or Zen, whether you call it existence, nothingness, nonexistence, non-nothingness, non-non-existence or non-non nothingness, whether you call it self, master, kōan, karma, or nature, you are marking the place on the side of the ship where the sword fell into the ocean some time ago [planning to look for it there in the future].

If you were to suspend understanding through name and form now, and were to doubt sufficiently where you can neither name things nor penetrate their meaning easily, and like one who has died a great death, you were to stop the movement of the mind and do nothing, hence becoming one with everything, you would then suddenly penetrate enlightenment as if something had in an instant come alive out of lifelessness. Then you would understand the monk asking the ancient master, "What is this place where all the buddhas are free of their bodies?" as well as the answer, "The eastern mountain floating on the water."

To the Venerable Gekokaku

THE FOUR ELEMENTS[12] are without self. I am originally without a master. This masterless master is the body, and this selfless self is true nature. Body and nature are not two, and the ten thousand Dharmas are one. In this unity there are no sages and no ordinary people. Where can life, death, and nirvana come from? The merit of existence and nonexistence does not apply to this wondrous wisdom. How can words or silence, movement or stillness affect it? Just abandon the myriad Dharmas, discard reason, let go of loss and gain, good and bad, this instant, and return to yourself and look cuttingly—who is it that looks? When you thoroughly penetrate this, the clarity stands out as lacquer black as a coal goose standing in the snow.

To the Zen Priest Soku Hōjū

STUDENTS OF THE WAY should see directly into their inherent nature. Knowledge, ignorance, clarity, and confusion miss the point. Who is it that hears or doesn't hear; who is it that sees or doesn't see? If you can answer, you get thirty blows. If you can't answer, you get thirty blows. What can you do to become intimate [with your true nature] without committing this offense? The frost falls during the blazing heat of the sixth month, a severe cold comes that penetrates to the bone and you lose your hold on life. Then comes rebirth and immediate attainment. Though mountains, rivers, and the great earth are one with the self, and your understanding is like a golden-haired lion's,[13] you are still lost in the backwoods. If the potential [of the mind] is not independent of position, you will fall into the Sea of Poison. How can you understand the meaning of "advancing in total dynamic activity"? Do you understand what is meant by, "Hearing the sound of the bell at noon, you chew your food and put on your seven-piece robe"?[14] If you understand, what is it?

To the Venerable Tsubaki Anshu regarding Practice in a Hermitage

L iving in a hermitage is first actualized when you are able to know the master in charge. The four elements [i.e., this physical body] are like an empty hermitage. Who could be made the master of such a hermitage? If there is no one in charge, who could know the master that sees and hears? If there is a master, what form does he take? He is like a dead person having dropped both existence and nonexistence. The inauthentic heretical Zen, which considers the mind a vast emptiness, though it may be alive and active, is still a [confining] pit of liberation.

Knowledge is the guest. Lack of knowledge is also the guest. What is the true master of the hermitage? A [true] dragon does not have dragon's features. An iron saw dances the *sandai*.[15] Do you understand? If you still do not, it will be difficult to consume even a drop of water. What of the donations from devotees? Don't spare light or darkness; time waits for on one.

To the Temple Kanin:[16] Shun of Tetsuyo

THE GREAT WAY IS COMPLETELY FREE of the six sense organs and the six pollutants.[17] It is not based on names, form, words, or phrases. You should step back and examine yourself thoroughly at this moment. What is it that comes here seeking these Dharma words? When you turn the light directly within and see clearly, the pure magnificent Dharma body of the self will manifest, and there will be nothing other than you. This is referred to as one's potential to leave the body. One who is careless and of shallow aspiration holds back and considers these manifestations to be reality and cannot attain true understanding as a result. You should see that it is easy to leave the body, but it is difficult to follow this way of liberation. Tell me now, what is this way of liberation? When you meet a dead serpent on the road, don't kill it. Pile things in a bottomless basket and bring them back home. If you have not clearly understood this, it would be difficult to [justify] your consumption of a drop of water. You would be like one who spent his life in monk's clothing caring only for his own well-being. How would you be able to avoid the iron staff of the Venerable En (King of Hell)? The great matter of life and death is crucial. Impermanence comes upon us in a flash. You should prize each day and night. Time waits for no one.

To The Scribe Kozan Hōgi

THE WAY OF THE MONK is not anything unusual. Just look directly into your inherent nature and don't depend on words. Most important, throw out everything and purify your life. Don't let the desire to read widely and become clever divert you from developing the Dharma eye of the self. Cleverness is total ignorance, wide knowledge is a banner announcing its interference with the Dharma. An ancient master said, "Heresy, even with cleverness, is not wisdom. It is scattered mind." Another said, "Forget the thinking mind, and you approach the Way. Discriminate and the demons prosper."

The World-Honored One sat in zazen for six years. Reeds sprouted piercing his knees yet he didn't notice. He exhausted all thinking, forgot all rewards, and the great wisdom of his inherent nature was revealed. There was nothing to attain outside of "seeing into one's own nature is Buddhahood." Everyone is endowed with this nature. It is the master of seeing and hearing. Look directly! What is this self-nature? Who is the master of seeing and hearing? Return to your source and you will understand. The light will shine of its own accord and form will disappear. Return to yourself often and look deeply. In this true self there is no knowing. So, with this point in mind, how can you enter the Way?

The High Priest Mumon said to the congregation, "To obey the regulations and keep the rules is to tie yourself without a rope. Arbitrary selfishness is heresy and devilry. Becoming settled and quiet while the mind exists is the heretical Zen of silent illumination.

Doing as you will, neglecting relationships, you fall into the deep pit of liberation. To be clever and clearheaded is to be tied in chains, to be bound in shackles. To think of good and bad is to dwell in the temples of heaven and hell. Fixed views of the Buddha and the Dharma enclose you in the two iron mountains.[18] One who has an instant awakening from an arising thought is sporting with spirits. Meditation in complete stillness is an activity of a demon. When you advance, you are deluded by Buddhist principles; when you retreat, you act contrary to Buddhist teachings. When you can neither advance nor retreat, you are a breathing corpse. Now, how on earth can you practice this after all? Work hard toward enlightenment in this life or regret it for an eternity."

This old master's compassionate teaching is broad. He takes students of the Way by the hand and teaches them. For the first time you can attain this subtle Way. But if you miss it by a hair's width the difference is as great as that between heaven and earth.

Well, do you understand? If you do, I'll give you thirty blows. If you don't, I'll give you thirty blows. Who is it that receives these blows? Quickly focus your attention! It's like saving your head. You are already late. If you don't understand, Venerable En, king of the underworld, will stand before you in judgment with a ball of molten iron for you to lick. How will you avoid the shame of this demon mind? Don't waste your time! Time waits for no one.

A Response to an Urgent Request from the Head of Shōbō Hermitage

I PONDERED ONE THING from the time I was a young boy. Who was it that responded "me" when I was asked, "Who are you?" Carrying this question without resolve, the years went by, until one day I decided to become a monk. At that time a great vow welled up inside of me. If I am going to be a monk, I will not seek liberation for myself alone. All the buddhas realized the Great Way to save ordinary people before seeking enlightenment for themselves. As long as I haven't resolved my doubts, I thought, I would neither study Buddhist texts nor learn the rituals practiced in Buddhist monasteries. While living in this world, I would seek out good teachers and spend my time deep in the mountains.

After becoming a monk, my doubt grew. At that time, I deepened my resolve to fulfill this vow to save ordinary people. I would do so by arousing the great "Way seeking mind" at a time when Shakyamuni Buddha was no longer in this world and the future buddha had not yet arrived. Even if I were to fall into the deepest darkest hell for my deluded feelings and views, I would suffer for the sake of ordinary people, never retreating through countless births into the distant future, never losing sight of my vow. I would not languish over concerns of life and death nor would I slack one bit, reveling in the practice of good deeds. Furthermore, I would not blind people, teaching them of the benefits of a Way, which I myself hadn't the power to attain.

I couldn't let go of this vow though it became an obsession that plagued my practice. Not being able to drop it, I appealed to all the buddhas, continuing my practice through thick and thin under the watchful eyes of divas until this day.

Though my account is of little value, I tell you of these delusions of my world in response to your strong request. I have written above for you to see this vow I've held since the beginning of my quest.

Notes

INTRODUCTION

1. Most of the information on Bassui's life presented here comes from *Nihon no zen goroku*, vol. II, edited by Furuta Shoken (Tokyo: Kodansha Press, 1979); *Nihon shisō taikei*, vol. 16, Chūsei zen no shisō, edited by Ichikawa Hakugen (Tokyo: Iwanami Shoten, 1970); Omori Sōgen, *Zen no kōsō* (Tokyo: Shunjūsha Press, 1979); *The Three Pillars of Zen*, edited by Philip Kapleau (Boston: Beacon Press, 1967).

2. Perhaps he was left with the understanding that the servant would pick him up; in this case he would have been abandoned only in a formal sense in order to fend off the evil spirits.

3. The paths of beings in hell, hungry ghosts, and animals.

4. It would seem from this statement that neither Bassui nor Tokukei was satisfied with the verification Bassui received from Kōzan Mongo.

5. Chūhō Myōhon (Chinese: Chung-feng Ming-pen) was noted as a recluse from Tenmokuzan in China who advocated a blend of Pure Land teaching and Zen.

6. Referring to Kohō by using the name of his temple.

7. Gasan Jōseki (1275–1365) was born in Kaga province (Ishikawa prefecture). He studied under Keizan Jōkin in the Daijoji Temple in Ishikawa. In 1324, he became chief priest of the Sōjiji Temple.

8. I have used Chang Chung-Yuan's translation from the *Original Teachings of Ch'an Buddhism*, p. 271.

9. I have used Sasaki's translation of *The Record of Linchi*, p. 8.

10. I have used Thomas Cleary's translation of the *Transmission of Light* (pp. 225–26).

11. See Steve Heine, *Dōgen and the Kōan Tradition*.

12. See Sōtō Zen in *Medieval Japan* by William M. Bodiford to understand the politics around Dōgen's Zen.

PART I

1. *Zenkyō:* two main doctrinal divisions of Buddhism from the standpoint of the Zen sect. One school depends on the inner experience of the Buddha and is directly transmitted from the Buddha's mind without relying upon scripture. The other school has a doctrinal system based upon the Buddha's teaching, such as the Kegon sect and the Tendai sect.

2. Bassui is here referring to Ch'an teaching in southern China. The Five Schools were Lin-chi (Japanese: Rinzai), Kuei-yang (Igyō), Ts'au-tung (Sōtō), Yün-mên (Ummon), and Fa-yen (Hōgen). The Lin-chi was divided into three branches: the original Lin-chi, Yang-ch'i (Yōgi), and Huang-lung (Oryū). These were the Seven Sects of Chinese Ch'an.

3. Hell, the realm of hungry spirits, and the realm of beasts.

4. Eyes, ears, nose, tongue, body, and mind.

5. Color and shape (Sanskrit: *rūpa*), sound *(śabda)*, perfume *(gandha)*, flavors *(rass)*, touch *(spraṣṭavya)*, and phenomena *(dharma)*.

6. Seeing, hearing, smelling, tasting, sensing, and being.

7. Yung-chia Hsüan-chüeh (Japanese: Yōka Genkaku; 675–713), one of the chief disciples of Hui-neng, the sixth ancestor of Ch'an Buddhism. The quote is from his "Song of Enlightenment" (Chinese: Cheng-tao Ke; Japanese: Shōdōka).

8. The same as the six pollutants. See note 5 above.

9. Mahākāśyapa was one of the ten major disciples of the Buddha. He is said to have become an arhat after being with the Buddha for only eight days. He devoted himself to the practice of *zuda-gyō* (the twelve-fold practice of the Theravada monk, which aims at eliminating all forms of attachment) and was regarded as the chief of the order.

10. The only one of the ten major disciples of the Buddha who is said to have understood emptiness.

11. This quote is found in the twenty-ninth chapter of the *Records of the Transmission of the Lamp* (Chinese: *Ch'uan-teng Lu;* Japanese: *Keitoku-dentō-roku*), a thirty-fascicle work composed by Tao-haüan of China in 1004. It describes the lineage of the Ch'an sect from the seven buddhas of the past to Wen-i, founder of the Fa-yen school.

12. See *Rinzai-roku (Record of Lin-chi)*, Iwanami Bunko edition, p. 47, "the four light functions."

13. This quote is in the *Gotōkaigen,* chapter 12.

14. See *Record of Lin-chi*, Discourse 8 (Sasaki translation): "One is endlessly on the way, yet has never left home. Another has left home, yet is not on the way."

15. *The Lotus Sutra* (Sanskrit: *Saddharma pundarika Sutra;* Japanese: *Myōhō renge-kyō*).

16. From Jōkaku's commentary on the Prajñāpāramitā Sutra.

17. Magical formulas, like mantras, which convey the essence of the teaching of sutras.

18. These are the last twelve stages of fifty-two in the T'ien-tai school. The ten stages are: joy at benefiting oneself and others, freedom from all possible defilement, emission of light and wisdom, glowing wisdom, overcoming utmost difficulty, realization of wisdom, proceeding far, attainment of immobility, attainment of expedient wisdom, ability to spread the teachings over the *dharma-dhātu* as clouds cover the sky. The two awakenings are: equivalent enlightenment and marvelous enlightenment.

19. See *Awakening of Faith in Mahāyāna* (Chinese: *Ta-ch'eng ch'i-hsin lun;* Japanese: *Daijō Kishinron*) for details of primary illusions.

20. The delusions caused by the six sense organs.

21. From the "Song of Enlightenment" by Yung-chia Hsüan-chüeh (see note 7).

22. *Sutra of Brahma's Net* (Japanese: *Bonmo-kyō*).

23. Ibid.

24. The laws governing the nation.

25. The six realms in which the souls of living beings transmigrate from one to another: the realms of hungry spirits, beasts, fighting demons, humans, heavenly beings, and the hell realm.

26. A term used for a bodhisattva who has reached the forty-eighth stage or greater.

27. A term used for a sentient being of superior quality; *sattva* (Japanese: *satta)* stands for sentient beings.

28. The sutra of the bodhisattva Jizō is not part of the Daizō-kyō (the traditional Buddhist canon), one reason for which is that it was probably written in China.

29. Though this story appears in the *Records of Nan-chüan,* Bassui probably took it from the *Record of Lin-chi* (see the Sasaki translation, Discourse 10).

30. *Zenyū,* also called an advanced friend, means a good teacher.

31. *Diamond Sutra.*

32. "Song of Enlightenment" (see note 7).

33. The seven buddhas that are said to have appeared in the world before the historical Buddha.

34. The eight Japanese sects of Bassui's day were the Ritsu (or Vinaya), Hossō, Tendai, Shingon, Zen, Kegon, Jōdō (Pure Land), and Jōdō Shin (True Pure Land) sects.

35. Morning, afternoon, evening, and three periods during the night.

36. Seshin (fourth century C.E.) is said to have written one thousand books. At first a follower of the Hināyāna teachings and critic of the Mahāyāna, he was influenced deeply by Asaṅga (Japanese: Mujaku) and hence converted to Mahāyāna. The Mahāyāna teachings that were expounded by Mujaku and Seshin were called the Yogacara School.

37. The wild fox is a metaphor for one who, not having been enlightened, acts as though he were a realized man, deluding everyone he meets.

38. Engo Kokugon (Chinese: Yuan-wu K'o-ch'in; 1083–1135) was the compiler of the *Blue Cliff Record* (Chinese: *Cho Pi Yan Lu;* Japanese: *Hekigan-roku).* The quote is from the fifteenth case.

39. *Tōzan Ryōkai* (Chinese: Tung-shan Liang-hsuan; 807–69). This quote is from the *Records of Tōzan*.

40. Said to be a disciple of the Buddha and also said to be the Buddha's son. Eliminating delusions from the world of desire, he reached the fourth stage of meditation; associating with evil persons, he developed wrong views; and planning to harm the Buddha, he fell into hell.

41. These quotes are attributed to Bodhidharma by the *Ketsumyaku-ron*.

42. This statement refers to the priest Gozu (594–657) to whom heavenly beings are said to have offered flowers while he was doing zazen on the northern cliff of Gozu Mountain. After meeting the fourth ancestor Dōshin (580–651), he had enlightenment and the heavenly beings are said to have stopped coming.

43. *The Heart Sutra* (Japanese: *Hannya-shin-gyō*) belonging to the Prajñāpāramitā literature.

44. Literally, causing chaos inside your stomach.

45. *"Totsu!"* is a Zen shout.

46. From the hundredth case of the *Blue Cliff Record* (see note 38). A monk asked Haryō, "What is the Blown-Hair Sword?" Haryō replied, "Each branch of the coral holds up the moon."

47. In Setchō's notes on this case we see: "The light engulfs myriad forms, the entire land." This is different from Bassui's statement but the sense is the same.

PART II

1. An arhat is one who has attained the fourth and final stage of enlightenment, a Theravadin Buddhist "saint."

2. See note 18 in Part I.

3. The second chapter of the *Lotus Sutra* entitled "Tactfulness." The literal translation is: "Only a Buddha together with a Buddha can really penetrate completely."

4. North, south, east, west, the four intermediate points of the compass, plus the above and below—that is, everywhere.

5. The *Sukhāvatī-vyūha, Aparimitāyus-sūtra,* often called the *Larger Sukhāvatīvyūha,* is one of the three sutras of Pure Land teaching according to Hōnen.

6. The ten evil deeds: killing, stealing, committing adultery, lying, using immoral language, slandering, equivocating, coveting, anger, and false views. The five deadly sins: killing one's father, killing one's mother, killing a saint *(arhat),* injuring the body of a buddha, and causing disunity in the community of monks.

7. *Lotus Sutra,* chapter 3 ("A Parable").

8. The *Amitāyur-dhyāna Sūtra,* one of the three Pure Land sutras according to Hōnen.

9. The Three Amida divinities (Japanese: Amida sanzon), Amida Buddha and his two attendants, Kannon Bodhisattva and Seishi Bodhisattva, are believed to welcome the departed into the Pure Land.

10. The *Vimalakīrti-nirdeśa Wūtra* (Japanese: *Yuima-gyō*), the story of a layman who remains a householder Buddhist and yet attains the wisdom of a bodhisattva.

11. *Record of Lin-chi.*

12. *Enlightenment Sutra* (Japanese: *Nehan-gyō*), chapter 14.

13. *Diamond Sutra* (Japanese: *Kongō-kyō*), chapter 5.

14. *Skandhas:* form, feeling, perception, volition, and consciousness.

15. *Vimalakīrti-nirdeśa Sūtra.*

16. *Avataṃsaka Sūtra* (Japanese: *Kegon-kyō*), chapter 6.

17. See note 3 of Introduction.

18. *Sutra of Eternal Life* (Japanese: *Muryōju-kyō*).

19. Sun, water, earth, trees, eight precious lakes of the Pure Land, heavenly towers, the lotus seat, image of Amida Buddha, views of all forms of Amida Buddha, Kannon Bodhisattva, Seishi Bodhisattva, seeing all heaven and buddhas, various images, the top three classes of the reborn,

the middle three classes of the reborn, and the lower three classes of the reborn.

20. The same as the six realms; see note 25 in Part I.

21. The four holy states: *śrāvaka, pratyekabuddha,* bodhisattva, and buddha. A śrāvaka (literally, "one who hears" the voice of Buddha and reaches enlightenment) is the lower of the four holy states. A pratyekabuddha is one who attains Buddhahood through independent practice, without a teacher.

22. *Diamond Sutra,* chapter 5.

23. The herdsman stands for the Buddha; the ten bodies are his attributes. There are different lists in different sutras. One such list is: Buddha of No attachment, Buddha Vowing to Save All Beings, Wisdom Buddha, Positive Buddha, Nirvana Buddha, Dharma Buddha, Mindful Buddha, Samadhi Buddha, Nature Buddha, and Easy Buddha.

24. *Diamond Sutra,* chapter 26 ("The Body of Truth Has No Marks").

25. Yung-chia Hsüan-chüeh (see note 7 in Part I). The quote is from the "Song of Enlightenment." The full quote is: "The heretics are clever but not wise; the fools [are] the childish ones—they suppose there is something in an empty fist."

26. This allusion refers to the Chinese scholars around the time of Confucius.

27. See note 34 in Part I.

28. Confucianism, Buddhism, and Taoism.

29. Tokusan Senkan (789–865) began practice solely as a scholar of the *Diamond Sutra,* writing extensive commentaries on it. Only later did he experience realization under Master Ryūtan Sōshin, and at this time he gave up his scholarship to devote himself to meditation. The story that follows is from Master Engo's commentary in the fourth case of the *Blue Cliff Record.*

30. The word for a bite to eat in Chinese, *tenjin,* literally means "to light up the mind."

31. Obai Kōnin (Chinese: Hung-yen; 602–75), the fifth ancestor in the lineage of the Chinese Ch'an sect.

32. See note 2 in Part I.

33. See note 40 in Part I.

34. The hell of "no interval" *(avici)* or uninterrupted hell—the last of the eight great hot hells, whose sufferers die and are reborn continuously.

35. Bodairushi Sanzō (Bodhiruci; ca. 535). A North Indian and contemporary of Bodhidharma who translated many scriptures into Chinese. He is regarded as the founder of the Jiron (Chinese: Ti-lun) sect and is also considered one of the ancestors of the Jōdō (Ching-t'u) sect.

36. Ruyaku (452–535)—a teacher who had thorough knowledge of sutras, sastras, and precepts.

37. That is, understanding even a particle of the true meaning of the sutras.

38. From the "Song of Enlightenment"; see note 7 in Part I.

39. *Koka* (Sanskrit: *kalpagni*)—the great fire that occurs at the end of the kalpa (aeon), destroying the universe.

40. From the *Record of Lin-chi*. Lin-chi said, "Look at the wooden puppets performing on stage. Their jumps and jerks all depend on the man behind."

41. See note 3 in Part I.

42. *Sutra on Perfect Enlightenment* (Japanese: *Engaku-kyō*).

43. *Diamond Sutra,* chapter 32 ("The Delusion of Appearances").

44. *Bodai* (Sanskrit: *bodhi*) usually means wisdom, Way, and enlightenment. It can also mean, as in this case, prayers for the deceased.

45. The Five Mountains and Ten Monasteries (Japanese: Gozanjissatsu) is a system of official Ch'an monasteries established in Sung-dynasty China, which in turn is said to have derived from an early Indian Buddhist system of five monasteries and ten pagodas. Japanese Rinzai Zen adopted this system during the Muromachi period.

46. From the "Song of Enlightenment."

47. Yung-chia Hsüan-chüeh; the quote is from the "Song of Enlightenment."

48. Kyōgen Chikan (?–898), a disciple of Isan Reiyū (771–853), was a

scholar of great erudition. Unable to answer Isan's question as to what his real self was, he burned all his books and left the master. He took up a job as grave-keeper and later heard a stone strike a bamboo and was instantly enlightened.

49. Reiun Shigon was a disciple of Isan.

50. Though Gensha Shibi (835–908) and Seppō Gison (822–908) were fellow disciples, Gensha regarded Seppō as his teacher and eventually succeeded him. He was a fisherman until he was thirty and is said to have been illiterate. Once, on a pilgrimage visiting Zen teachers, he stumbled on a stone and stubbed his toes. He felt a great pain penetrate his entire being and at that moment was enlightened.

51. Black beans signify words. Hence the meaning: You will spend your life touching the surface of words without understanding their substance.

52. Kyōshō Dōshin (868–973) was a disciple of Seppō. The story is in the forty-sixth case of the *Blue Cliff Record*.

53. See note 37.

54. Ummon Bunen (864–949): a noted master who used vigorous language and violent tactics to awaken his disciples. He was a disciple of Seppō.

55. *Lotus Sutra*, chapter 2 ("Faith and Discernment").

56. The questioner's summary of this story from the "Faith and Discernment" chapter of the *Lotus Sutra* (chapter 14) is as follows: "The rich man's son who left his home with no particular purpose, forgetting his father and separating from his family." I have translated freely here to follow the text of the sutra. See *The Threefold Lotus Sutra,* translated by Bunnō Katō, Yoshirō Tamura, and Kōjirō Miyasaki (New York: Weatherhill/Kosei, 1975), p. III.

57. This is a quote taken from the *Diamond Sutra,* chapter 14 ("Perfect Peace Lies in Freedom from Characteristic Distinctions").

58. *Lotus Sutra* (the chapter titled "Tactfulness").

59. The term Avatamsaka Manifold comes from the *Avatamsaka* or *Flower Wreath Sutra* (Japanese: *Kegon*). It refers to the concept of "realms" described in this sutra, which are set up for meditation in the Kegon school.

60. The Buddha of Healing (Japanese: Yakushi-nyorai, Sanskrit: Bhaiṣajya-guru)

61. (Japanese: Fugen-bosatsu; Sanskrit: Samantabhadra-bodhisattva). The Bodhisattva who typifies the teaching, meditation, and practice of the Buddha. He is the right-hand attendant of the Shakyamuni Buddha, mounted on a white elephant.

62. (Japanese: Monju-bosatsu; Sanskrit: Mañjuśri-bodhisattva). The Bodhisattva of meditation and wisdom. The left-hand attendant of the Shakyamuni Buddha, mounted on a lion.

63. *Sutra of Perfect Enlightenment.*

64. Covetousness, anger, and foolishness.

65. *Diamond Sutra,* chapter 7 ("No Merit, No Discourse").

66. Ibid.

67. *Diamond Sutra,* chapter 10 ("Sublime Pure Land").

68. Kannon (Sanskrit: Avalokiteśvara)—the bodhisattva who vows to save all beings through the power of compassion.

69. *Lotus Sutra,* chapter 8 ("The Universal Gate").

70. Daijō (Sanskrit: Mahāyāna), the Great Vehicle to enlightenment is one of the two original schools of Buddhism. Its attitude is somewhat more liberal than Shojō (Sanskrit: Hināyāna), the Small Vehicle. Hināyāna is a term coined by the Mahāyāna Buddhists and not appreciated by the former school.

71. At the Deer Park at Isipatana (modern Sarnath) near Benares, India, the Buddha delivered his first sermon. The Hiranyarati Rivers runs through Kusinagara (modern Uttar Pradesh), where the Buddha passed away.

72. See note 9 in Part I.

73. A cousin of the Buddha, his favorite disciple and constant attendant for the last twenty years of his life.

74. From a poem entitled "Sandōkai" ("In Praise of Identity") by Sekitō Kisen (Chinese: Shih-t'ou Hsi-ch'ien; 700–790).

75. *Ui* (Sanskrit: saṃskṛta): "that which is made." *Ui* refers to phenomena produced through causation.

76. See note 3 in the introduction.

77. The sense is the same as the three evil paths. I don't know why Bassui added a fourth—fighting demons—here.

78. Bassui's strong condemnation of the drinking of alcohol suggests how widespread the problem was in monasteries of that time.

79. *Sutra of the Brahma's Net.*

80. The *Sōgo Sutra on Cause and Effect.* This sutra is not part of the Daizō-kyō (the traditional Buddhist canon).

81. *Record of My Reflections* (Japanese: *Shakumon Jikyō no Roku*) in three volumes, edited by Kaishin.

82. Shae (Sanskrit: Srāvastī) the capital of Kosala, is the location of the Jeta-vana Grove and site of the first Buddhist monastery where the Buddha and his followers used to spend the rainy season.

83. Embudai (Sanskrit: Jambu-Dvīpa) is the name of a great island to the south of Mount Sumeru—according to the traditional cosmological view, the world in which we are living.

84. The sixth of the seven buddhas said to have lived before the appearance of the historical Buddha.

85. These virtues relate to monks who receive the precepts. They are: entering nirvana and frightening demons, receiving alms, living a pure life, keeping the precepts, and eliminating evil.

86. Things allotted for temple use such as daily utensils, food given to monks traveling outside the temple, donations given to temples for resident monks, and donations brought to temples for monks invited from the ten directions.

87. Meaning a layman, since most householders dressed in white.

88. A senior monk.

89. Rules of discipline and community living for Buddhist monks, con-

tained in the first of three collections or "baskets" comprising the Buddhist canon.

90. See note 34 in Part I.

91. The images of the nine-tailed fox and the golden-tailed lion were taken from the *Engo Shinyō (Important Pointers from Master Engo,* completed in 1145), which depicts two mythical creatures: one a trickster (the fox) and the other a king (the lion). The golden tail may symbolize satori. Was Bassui contrasting the two modes of practice—studying the eight sects with penetrating the one mind?

PART III

1. Here dharma refers to the path one chooses and not necessarily the Buddha dharma.

2. Gozu Hōyū (Chinese: Niu-t'ou Fa-jung; 594–657) was a disciple of the fourth patriarch, Dōshin. Gozu is the name of the mountain where he lived. He was founder of the Niu-t'ou school.

3. I use the expression "Dharma combat" for the Japanese *issatsu* (literally, challenge). The ritualized Dharma combat at Zen temples today is *hossen.*

4. Baso Do'itsu (Chinese: Ma-tsu Tao-i; 709–788) was a disciple of Nangaku Ejō. Baso's teaching, originally propagated in the province of Chiang-hsi, had great influence in the Buddhist world of the time, and it was through his influence that Zen Buddhism took root in China.

5. One *ri* is six hundred meters.

6. From the "Song of Enlightenment."

7. A watō is a statement of an encounter between Zen master and student, in baffling language, pointing to the truth. Traditionally the watō was the response while the whole encounter was the kōan.

8. These are five Zen monks known for their eccentricity; the first three were wandering monks.

9. Presumably meat.

10. There is a story similar to this in Dōgen in *Zuimonki*. Dogen was warning against judging one by his actions without first giving careful consideration to all the circumstances. Here Bassui uses this quote perhaps to show that monks like Chotō may have acted in eccentric ways but there was more to their actions than we can fully comprehend.

11. This story appears as the sixth case of the *Mumonkan* ("The Gateless Gate").

12. See note 50 in Part II. The ancient master is Gensha Shibi.

13. Nansen Fugan (Chinese: Nan Ch'uan; 748–834). The quote is from the twenty-fifth case of the *Blue Cliff Record.*

14. See note 31 in Part II.

15. Taigan Enō (Chinese: Hui-neng; 638–713), the sixth patriarch in the lineage of Chinese Zen.

16. From the twenty-fifth case of the *Blue Cliff Record.* According to this case the response is by Setcho and not Nansen.

17. *Myōkon (jīvitendriya),* translated as life-root, is one of the cittaviprayukta-saṃskāras. According to the Abbi-dharma-kośa (Japanese: *Kusha-ron*), jīvita means duration of life *(āyus)* or the measure of life allotted to a person. In this context it seems to mean attachment to living a long life.

18. The character *rei* usually translates as spirit or soul but is here translated as essential nature.

19. Sōzan Honjaku (840–901) was a disciple of Tōzan Ryōkai.

20. Chōsha Keishin (dates unknown) was a disciple of Nansen Fugan. This quote is taken from the *Transmission of the Lamp,* vol. 10.

21. (Chinese: Wu-men Hui-kai, 1183–1260), compiler of the *Mumonkan* (*Wu-men Kuan* in Chinese), was the teacher of Shinchi Kakushin who in turn was the teacher of Kohō Kakumyō, Bassui's teacher.

22. According to Buddhist mythology, there are nine mountain ranges around Mount Sumeru, the center of the universe. The outermost range—the two iron mountains—symbolizes the borders of the universe.

23. From the *Mumonkan*, Mumon's Zen warnings. See Zenkei Shibayama, *Zen Comments on the Mumonkan,* translated by Sumiko Kudo (New York: Harper & Row, 1975), p. 332.

24. The last part of Mumon's quote from the previous paragraph was left out by Bassui. It is as follows: "Finish it in this life. Don't let yourself suffer an eternal karmic debt." The inclusion of this part would give more meaning to the statement by Bassui that follows.

25. The withered tree stands for the quiet empty mind. See Furuta Shōken's notes in *Nihon no Zen no goroku,* vol. II, p. 365.

26. Crossing the world of light and darkness (that is, relativity); see Furuta Shōken's notes, p. 369.

27. Having no passion for the Way; see Furuta Shōken's notes, p. 370.

28. The Buddha met with twenty-five hundred people and addressed the bodhisattva Dṛdhamati, describing the meditation named Śūramgama. The substance of the talk makes up the *Śūramgama Sutra.*

29. See note 17 in Part I.

30. *Śūramgama Sutra,* the verse in chap. 6.

31. *Jōdō,* a term in Zen monasteries for the entrance of the chief abbot into the lecture hall to give a lecture; also the entrance of priests into the meditation hall to take a meal.

32. This is a quote from the first case of the *Blue Cliff Record.* It is a line from the master Engo's verse warning against dwelling on recollections.

33. See page 152 of the text.

34. See note 7 in Part III.

35. Fuzan Hōen (991–1067). The quote is from the commentary to the hundredth case of the *Blue Cliff Record.*

36. This quote, from Baso, appears in the thirtieth case of the *Mumonkan.*

37. Hyakujō Ekai (Chinese: Pai-chang; 749–814), a disciple of Baso.

38. Kanchi Sōsan (Chinese: Sêng-ts'an; ?–606), the third patriarch in the lineage of Chinese Zen. The quote is from the Shinjinmei (Chinese: Hsinsin-ming).

39. This passage is from the first case of the *Mumonkan*. Mumon is commenting on a classic kōan: A monk asked Jōshū, "Has a dog Buddha-nature?" Jōshū answered, *"Mu."* *Mu* literally means "no," but the response is not to be taken literally. The student is asked to think *mu,* but to think from this that the answer is that a dog does not have Buddha-nature would be a mistake.

40. Ryūge Kodon (835–923), a disciple of Tozan Ryōkei. The quote is from the twentieth case of the *Blue Cliff Record.*

41. This quote from Goso Hōen (?–1104) makes up the thirty-eighth case of the *Mumonkan.*

42. A word that awakens (turns their minds from delusion to satori).

43. These words are attributed to Kassan Zenne (805–80).

44. This comes from the four guest–host relationships attributed to Tōzan Ryōkai. Guest stands for use (discrimination); host stands for essence body (equality).

45. This phrase comes from the fortieth case of the *Blue Cliff Record.* Engo's introduction starts, "Stop the mind and an iron tree blooms with flowers."

46. The complete story is as follows: Two monks in the assembly of the master Yin Tsung, seeing a pennant blown about in the wind, argued as to what was in motion, the wind or the pennant. The sixth patriarch, hearing this, said it was neither the wind nor the pennant but rather the mind that moves. The assembly of monks was startled by the sixth patriarch's statement. This story can be found in both the *Platform Sutra* of the sixth patriarch and in the twenty-ninth case of the *Mumonkan.*

47. This quote comes from the *Transmission of the Lamp.* The original translates as: "You should know that none of the many interpretations is correct." The original seems to make more sense in light of the sentence that follows.

48. Suigan Kashin (dates unknown), a disciple of Sekisō Soen (986–1039).

49. Jimyō, another name for Sekisō Soen (ibid).

50. This is from the seventh volume of the *Transmission of the Lamp.* The clouds stand for delusion; the moon stands for reality or enlightenment.

51. Tōzan Shusho (910–990), a disciple of Ummon Bunen (864–949).

52. Engo (Chinese: Yuan-wu; 1063–1165). The quote is from Engo's pointer to the twenty-fifth case of the *Blue Cliff Record.*

53. Referring to the eastern and western halls of the temple. The meaning is that a Zen monk walks freely right here and now.

54. Compare the Zen master Baso's reply to the question, "Who is the man who does not take all things as his companions?" Baso: "I will tell you after you have swallowed all the water in the West River."

55. The broken mirror stands for enlightenment.

56. Daie Sōkō (1089–1163), a disciple of Engo.

57. The skin pouch stands for the body.

58. *Danken* in Japanese (Sanskrit: *uccheda-dṛṣṭi*): the doctrine of annihilation; the teaching that death marks the final end of the individual with no survival of any sort; the opposite of eternalism (Japanese: *jōken*).

59. *Nijo no danken* in Japanese. Heretical views of two types: vehicle of hearing—one is enlightened after hearing the teaching from a master; vehicle of inclination for awakening—the principles of Dharma are understood and one is enlightened without hearing the formal Buddhist teaching. According to Mahāyāna thinking, both examples are self-serving and thus contradictory to the bodhisattva ideal.

60. *Jōken* in Japanese (Sanskrit: *śāśvata-dṛṣṭi*): the doctrine of eternity; the notion that the world is eternal; eternalism, in which the conditioned elements are eternal. This doctrine is based on the theory of the *ātman*, which is falsely perceived as eternal.

61. This transformation body is expressed in the *Sutra of Perfect Enlightenment.* The bodhisattva with the power of prayer enters various societies, changing his form to save ordinary people.

62. The heretical view that since everything is natural there is no need to do anything—no need to practice, listen to the teachings, and so forth.

63. Ummon Bunen (864–949). "If I had seen it" refers to the Buddha's action right after birth: taking seven steps in the four directions and pointing to the heavens, and so on.

64. Godaisan (Chinese: Wu-t'ai-shan): a mountain range in Shan-si province in China famed for its many Buddhist temples. The first Indian monks who came to China are said to have lived there. This site is said to be the abode of Maitreya Bodhisattva.

65. The Japanese characters for bird and horse are similar.

PART IV

1. See note 3 in Part I.

2. The ten evil deeds (*jūaku* in Japanese) are killing, stealing, committing adultery, lying, using immoral or flippant language, slandering, equivocating, coveting, becoming angry, and holding false views. The five cardinal sins (*gogyaku* in Japanese) are killing one's father, killing one's mother, killing a saint, injuring the body of a buddha, and causing disunity in the community.

3. See note 7 in Part I.

4. The three worlds of delusion: the worlds of greed, form, and formlessness.

5. This sentence seems probably to be Bassui's way of indicating transcendence of logical thinking.

6. The realm of hell, hungry ghosts, fighting demons, beasts, humans, and heavenly beings.

7. *Cintōmani* in Sanskrit, and *nyoihōju* in Japanese, refers to a fabulous gem capable of responding to every wish.

8. (Sanskrit: Ksitigarbha) Jizō is a bodhisattva who is venerated in folk belief as a savior from the torments of hell and helper of deceased children. (See "The Bodhisattva Jizō," p. 30, above.)

9. See note 61 in Part II.

10. The high seat in this case indicates a senior monk or teacher who takes the lecturer's seat.

11. In Buddhist mythology, the ruler of hells.

12. The four elements are earth, water, air, and fire.

13. A golden-haired lion is symbolic of an able monk, advanced in his understanding of the Dharma. The Bodhisattva Manjushri is pictured riding a lion.

14. In the sixteenth case of the *Mumonkan*, the master Ummon says, "The world is vast and wide. Why do you put on your seven-piece robe at the sound of the bell?" The bell is rung to inform the monks of the last morning meal after which they can't eat that day. Ummon is asking them why they obediently respond to the bell if they are really free in the absolute "vast and wide world."

15. *Sandai* is the name of a traditional Japanese dance.

16. A *kanin* is a person in charge of the administration of a temple.

17. See notes 4 and 5 in Part I.

18. See note 22 in Part III.

Index

Wisdom Publications

WISDOM PUBLICATIONS, a not-for-profit publisher, is dedicated to preserving and transmitting important works from all the major Buddhist traditions as well as related East-West themes.

To learn more about Wisdom, or browse our books on-line, visit our website at wisdompubs.org. You may request a copy of our mail-order catalog on-line or by writing to:

WISDOM PUBLICATIONS
199 Elm Street
Somerville, Massachusetts 02144 USA
Telephone: (617) 776-7416
Fax: (617) 776-7841
Email: info@wisdompubs.org
www.wisdompubs.org

THE WISDOM TRUST

As a not-for-profit publisher, Wisdom is dedicated to the publication of fine Dharma books for the benefit of all and dependent upon the kindness and generosity of sponsors in order to do so. If you would like to make a donation to Wisdom, please do so through our Somerville office. If you would like to sponsor the publication of a book, please write or email us at the address above.

Thank you.

Wisdom is a nonprofit, charitable 501(c)(3) organization affiliated with the Foundation for the Preservation of the Mahayana Tradition (FPMT).